Born Dead on a Winter's Night

by

Rolland Love

Rolland Love

Born Dead on a Winter's Night
By
Rolland Love
All rights reserved. Copyright © 2017

This is a collection of memories that Rolland Love has written about moments or events, both public and or private that took place in his life from birth until he entered college. The assertions made in the work are understood to be factual. Born Dead on a Winter's Night is based on Love's experiences growing up in the Ozark Mountains.

Book Cover by Larry Bodinson and Paul Middleton
Photo's by Mike Overmyer

"There was never yet an uninteresting life. Such a thing is impossible. Inside of the dullest exterior there is a drama, a comedy, and a tragedy." --- Mark Twain.

Chapter 1

Born Dead

I was born dead, in the dead of winter, still as a stone. Blue as the smoky haze that sometimes settles on the Ozark Mountains. I know because my mother, Helen Love, my father Ray Love and Aunt Maude told me so. I can only imagine the scene: Doc Barnes, a tall rugged-looking man with bushy white hair, worked frantically when he realized there was trouble. His white shirt covered in blood and the flickering light of a kerosene lamp added ghost-like dimension to the scene. Cold enough to see your breath, the only source of heat came from a cast iron wood burning stove in the living room. I was saved because Doc carried me outside and rolled me in snow that covered the ground from a midwinter storm. The cold caused me to take a breath and I began to cry.

I'm pretty sure starting life dead has had an effect on me. Often, I feel or see or think about something and it stalks me. It might be a word, a name, an animal, or a place. This syndrome has been my companion since I was a kid.

Here's an example: "The first time I can remember something being different I was five years old. Before trouble raised its ugly head I had a feeling something bad was going to happen. I actually got a lump in my throat. Within minutes, a mean old Billy goat jumped the fence without me being aware, rammed into my backside, and knocked me down. I was covered in mud, but was not badly hurt. The experience set the stage for many premonitions and intuitions to come.

Up until now I've only talked to a few people about my frequent recalls. When I have, they said stuff like, "Hell, things like that happen to lots of people" so I quit saying anything about my mind being out of kilter. But I often felt a sense of knowing something was going to happen when I felt a lump in my throat.

That's the end of me talking about this for now; we've got other important things to investigate.

Chapter 2

Stomping Tomatoes and Fishing with Dad

I got my first spanking when I was four years old. I walked into the garden and stomped on a ripe tomato. I laughed as red juice squished between my toes. It felt like the muddy puddles in front of our house after a rain. Dad picked me up, carried me to a picnic table in the backyard and told me to stay put. As soon as he walked away I scampered back into the garden, stomped on another tomato and laughed even louder.

After the second offense, Dad swatted by my behind and said, "We don't stomp on food we need to eat." I cried and my dog Trouser, a black and tan hound we occasionally used when we hunted coons, licked away my tears. That was the only time my dad ever spanked me. Sometimes when I look at a tomato, even after all these years, I think about what happened. As it turned out, we had more tomatoes than we could eat that summer. Even though I was only four years old I learned a lesson about obedience; when my dad said to stop doing something, I did.

I was five years old when I caught my first fish. I hurried to keep up with my dad as we walked toward the pond close to our house, each carrying a cane pole with corncob bobbers tied on the line. Along the way, Dad caught half dozen brown grasshoppers with yellow wings to use as bait. He put them in the breast pocket of his blue denim overalls and snapped a button so they couldn't escape. When we arrived at the pond Dad threaded one on each of our hooks. Soon after we tossed our lines into the water my bobber disappeared under the surface and something was trying to pull the pole out of my hands.

3

"I've got a fish," I yelled.

"Hope it's not a snapping turtle," Dad said and he laughed.

As I walked backwards to drag the fish onto the bank I stumbled over Trouser and fell to the ground. As usual when I needed him to give me a lick on the face he gave me a couple.

"It's a big blue gill," Dad said. "Get a half dozen more fish this size we'll be eatin' high on the hog, so to speak."

During the next thirty minutes we caught a couple more bluegill, a largemouth bass and Dad caught a catfish, which weighed two pounds. After we got house, Dad skinned the cat and scaled the other fish. He chopped off their heads and gutted them. Mom rolled our catch in cornmeal and fried them crispy brown in a cast iron skillet on a wood-burning stove. Along with corn and potatoes from the garden, we had a feast for dinner.

In addition to a tasty meal, I loved the thrill of catching fish. The earth's beauty was intoxicating: the high-pitched melodious call of a red-winged blackbird swaying on a cattail stem, a bellowing bullfrog sitting on a lily pad under the shade of a willow tree, dragon flies with iridescent blue wings skimmed over the surface of the water. There had been a heavy fog early in the morning. The air smelled fresh, like after a summer rain. I had seen a rainbow in my mind as I awoke that morning and in only a couple miles in front of me blue, red and yellow colors in the form of a giant arch appeared. One of those mystical happenings that make you appreciate being alive.

Even though I was only five years old, I'll never forget what my Dad said, "Fishing jumpstarts the imagination. If you want to escape from the daily routine, go fish."

A couple days later I decided to fish on my own. I dug half dozen worms from the garden and put the brown, wriggling creatures in an empty red Prince Albert tobacco can. I picked up one of the cane poles Dad had stored beside the house. Before leaving the yard I threaded one of the worms on my hook. I wanted to be ready to fish when I reached the pond. With the line dangling from the end of the pole, I walked into the barn lot where a flock of clucking chickens pecked at some corn I had tossed on the ground earlier. I swung the baited hook in front of a Rhode Island Red rooster and he gobbled the worm in one swift peck.

When I raised the cane pole hoping the hook would dislodge, the rooster jumped five feet in the air. Feathers flew and half dozen hens clucked as they ran toward the big bird, which was obviously in distress. Dust billowed off the dry ground. The rooster was accustomed to being king of the flock but his life had changed the instant since I came along. The comfort of a dozen brightly feathered female companions, a newly constructed chicken house Dad built only a couple weeks earlier, and all the corn the big bird could eat was about to be something of the past. A streak of fear ran through me as the rooster fell to the ground, flopping and spinning like a top.

The backdoor slammed and my mother yelled at the top of her voice. "What's going on out here? Is that fox after the chickens again?"

I froze and told my first lie. "Old rooster chased me and tried to steal my worm."

"Looks like he caught it," Mom said. "He's hooked isn't he?"

Mom rushed to the smoke house and picked up a hatchet. She grabbed the rooster by his hind legs and, quick as she could carry him to a stump, chopped off his head. Blood flying from the severed neck, the headless body of the rooster flopped around out of control. There, for the entire world to see, poking out of the headless neck was my wriggling worm still on the hook.

"Don't dangle your worms in front of any more chickens, okay?" Mom took the rooster to a table by a water pump where we cleaned critters we had killed and wanted to eat.

Dad walked up, looked at the rooster and said, "I raised the old boy from a chick. Happy for him he got to tend to the flock for a number of years." He looked at me and shook his head, "Before somebody did him in."

"Go on an' fish," Mom said. "Take a stringer. If you catch enough we can have your grandpa and grandma over for dinner. They'd be proud to share your first catch. Don't worry about the rooster; everybody makes mistakes."

That was truly the temperament my mother had her entire life. It's one of those things where you look back and wish you had been a better person for her sake.

I caught five catfish weighing a couple pounds each. Even a bullfrog jumped off his lily pad and swallowed my worm. During the process, one of the sharp catfish horns stuck in the tip of my finger. Blood oozed and formed a red puddle on the table. I wiped it up before Mom could see it and say, "Be more careful."

The fish I caught impressed grandpa and Grandma. Sharing a big white platter with a half dozen ears of corn was fried fish and frog legs, a combination that was hard to beat. Grandma had baked a pie with apples from a tree in their front yard and I turned the handle on ice cream freezer to provide one of my favorite treats.

Chapter 3

Guarding Mom's Garden

On the first day of spring, I walked into the kitchen and sat down at the table to eat breakfast. Glad winter was over, it was bitter doing chores in the dark, so cold your breath looked like a cloud of frost.

The only thing that made a bitter morning tolerable was watching the sun come up over the ridge, shining through the open barn door. It painted mystical golden streaks across the wall. Like many things in our self-sufficient world. I didn't appreciate them when I was young. Like my mother used to say, "Why would we want to go on vacation, we already live in paradise. Soon, I would be swimming, diving off of tall limestone bluffs, floating the river and catching fish. Normally, Mom gave me a wink and a nod and Dad asked if I slept well. But this morning, they paid me no mind.

"Something wrong?" I asked.

Dad took a sip of coffee picked up his straw hat and said, "We're caught in a dry spell. If it don't rain soon we've got ourselves a pack of trouble."

"What kind of trouble?" I looked around and wondered how things could be much better. There were half dozen fried eggs on a platter with slices of ham, a couple of fried quail breast from a hunt the day before, a jar of honey, biscuits and a pitcher of milk.

Mom shook her head. "Nothing grows without water. We need hay and corn to feed the livestock. The milk cow needs grass to eat."

"No rain means scrawny vegetables in the garden," Dad said. "We need to store a lot of canned goods in the root cellar to get us though next winter. And we need corn for cornbread and mush and all those other dishes your mom makes for us out of cornmeal."

Mom reached across the table and patted the back of my hand. "I'll tell what you can do to help."

I straightened up in my chair. "What would that be?"

Mom got up and opened the oven door on a black cast-iron cook stove. The smell of cinnamon filled the air. She grabbed a dishtowel, lifted out a steaming apple pie, and set it on the cabinet next to the water bucket.

"Your job this summer is to stop the critters," Mom said. "We lose a lot of our food to them. This year we can't afford to lose any.

Grandma and Grandpa can no longer plant their own garden. Vegetables for both families will have to come from our patch."

"How can I stop them? Critters eat whatever they want."

Mom smiled, bowed her head, and started the breakfast prayer. "Lord, we thank you for the food and all your blessings. If you see fit to bring us some rain soon we'll appreciate it." Mom's voice quavered when she asked the Lord to keep Grandma and Grandpa safe, as well.

"Amen," Dad said. He forked a slice of ham, a quail breast and a couple of eggs onto his plate. He looked at me and raised his eyebrows. "Everybody has to pitch in during a time of need. The job of keeping critters from eating our food is all yours, son."

I started to say that everybody knows nobody can win against Mother Nature, and then decided it would do no good. For the first time ever I assumed a responsibility that made me know what it felt like to be a grown-up. When you live off the land and what you do affects people's lives, scaring away critters from the food supply is serious business.

I forked a biscuit onto my plate, spread on some butter, and coated it with honey. As I washed down the warm, sweet biscuit with milk, I thought about what kind of animals ate from our garden. The list was long. My job would be more than just building some dumb looking scarecrow. I would have to be a lot smarter to stop birds and animals from eating our food. I asked to be excused from the table.

"We'll help anyway we can," Dad said as I started out the door. "Your grandpa and grandma know a lot about keeping away varmints, too."

With a banging sound of the screen door ringing in my ears, I walked into the garden to survey the situation. I knew Mom would start planting in the next few days, so I had no time to dilly-dally around. From helping plant the garden in the past, the first seeds in the ground would be peas, carrots, beets, turnips, radishes, and potatoes. A week or so latter would come lettuce and cabbage, then tomato and pepper transplants. The last thing to get covered with dirt would be kernels of sweet corn, a favorite of deer, crows, blackbirds, Mom, Dad, Grandpa, Grandma, and me.

The next day was Saturday. I would tag along with Dad to the livestock sale barn. Figured I'd run into folks in addition to Grandpa and Ira who would have remedies, I needed to make a list of questions to ask while Dad and I did chores, milked the cow, sloped the hogs, fed the chickens, and gather eggs, we could talk about my plan to scout things out at the sale barn.

"That sounds like a great idea and the smartest thing you could do," Dad said. "Always good to have a plan."

I sat under an oak tree in the front yard with pencil and paper to list the names of all the critters I must keep out of the garden, starting with blackbirds and blue jays. Mr. Rabbit, the biggest nibbler of all was at the top of my list. Next were squirrels, raccoons, moles, crows, and deer. I drew pictures of the critters next to their names to make the project more interesting and that would help me find my place when I wanted to make a new note. Next to the pictures, I listed things I thought I would use so I could compare what I already knew to what I learned at the sale barn.

The next morning Mom made one of my favorites for breakfast, crispy-fried bacon and pancakes with chopped black walnuts mixed in the batter. I rolled the bacon into a pancake sandwich and filled it with melted butter and syrup.

After Dad and I finished chores, we headed to town in the pick-up. On the way, I pulled out my list and asked a couple of questions to see what he would say, compared to what I had written down.

"You ever heard of laying a few pieces of rubber hose around in the garden to keep out rabbits?" I asked.

The look on Dad's face indicated I should check that one off my list.

"You might fool a snake into falling in love," he said. "But I doubt you'd scare away rabbits. I've heard rabbits are scared of their own reflections. You might set mirrors around."

I crossed out rubber hose, wrote mirror, and put away my paper. When we pulled into the sale barn lot, I saw half dozen people whom I figured would know the best thing to do about critters, including Ira and Grandpa.

He seemed more stooped over every time I saw him and it made me sad. I walked up to ask him how to keep out birds.

He put his hand on my shoulder and steadied himself. "I hear you're gonna save the garden crops from critters this summer."

I smiled. "I figure you got some good advice. How am I going to keep away crows, black birds, and blue jays?"

"Whatever you do don't let them get into a daily feeding habit," Grandpa said, "Once they get a taste of a crop it's harder to chase them away. I bet you'd be the same?"

That seemed a bit strange. I waited for more.

Grandpa stroked his chin. "I'd build a scarecrow with lots of shiny buttons. Put a cowbell on it and tie that to a string. Every time a bird comes near the garden, pull the damned string."

"Great idea!" I said. "Only thing is, I can't sit out in the yard all day long."

"Tie the string to a tree branch, so when the wind blows, it rings the bell. Another thing you can do is tying some string across the garden. Birds don't like string strung around."

I could build a scarecrow to do just what Grandpa said without any trouble. I thanked him as I looked into his pale blue eyes. He walked away slowly with careful steps. He was such a kind person and helped many folks; I wished he would live forever.

My next critter to find out about was Mr. Rabbit. Uncle Ira would be the one to tell me what I should do about the most persistent pests of all. When I asked him, he seemed in a playful mood.

"The only way you can keep out rabbits is to dig a trench around the entire garden and fill it with water."

I knew he was kidding. "This is important stuff," I said. "If it don't rain we're going to need every carrot and ear of corn I can save."

He stepped back and grinned. "OK. Here's what you do. It's a bit of work, but it's the only sure way to keep 'em out. Put up a 2-foot-tall, chicken-wire fence with the bottom tight against the ground. The mesh needs to be 1 inch or smaller to stop young rabbits from going through. There'll be plenty of those little critters."

"Where can I get wire?" I asked. "And what about the post? How long will it take?"

Ira slapped me on the back and shook his head. "It won't take anytime at all. I'll help you. I'll even bring the wire. We can cut oak saplings from the woods for posts."

"Thank you," I said. "I need to do it quick."

"This afternoon soon enough?"

I nodded. "What about stopping squirrels?"

Uncle Ira pointed at Bill Thompson, the barber. "Go ask him."

"You could use a haircut," Bill said, the way he always did when he saw me. I let his comment slid and told him what was on my mind.

"I'll give you a big bag of hair. If you mix it into the soil, there will be no squirrels in the garden. They cannot stand the smell of humans."

I thanked him for the suggestion, but wondered if what he told me was right. I asked another man standing nearby.

"If Bill Thomson says it's so, it is," Jack Curtis said.

So I wrote "hair" to the side of my squirrel drawing.

Willie Simmons had the biggest truck patch garden in the county—5 acres or more. He grew watermelon, cantaloupe, pumpkin, and sweet corn, which he sold at the sale barn.

"You want to get rid of deer?" Willie asked when he heard me talking to Jack.

"I sure do," I said. I always liked the way Willie dressed. He looked like a farmer, a man of the earth. Bib overalls, red plaid shirt, straw hat that looked crusty as something he might have borrowed from a scarecrow and brogans soiled with barnyard manure.

"Smelly old shoes will do the trick. Put half dozen pair on top of tomato stakes, deer won't come near your garden. In this dry weather, I'd water them once a day so they'll smell to high heaven. I've seen hungry deer circle a pair of my old boots and never set one hoof inside my truck patch. The smell helps keep away birds, rabbits, and other critters, too."

My next worry was moles, which attack root crops. I'd seen them chew away a carrot under the ground, leaving the green tops looking good, but when I pulled it from the ground, nothing was left.

Reverend Leroy used to be a preacher—until he ran out of anything folks cared to hear him say. I asked him my next question, his big garden used to be the pride of his life. That was before he moved to a river called Big Creek and took up living in a cave.

I told him what I was up to. "How do I get rid of moles?"

"Why didn't you ask me about raccoons?" he said. So I did, which was a mistake. He got up close to my ear like he was whispering a secret his breath smelled bad as a dead skunk in the hot summer sun.

"Plant enough corn for both man and beast. The Lord will bless you for helping feed his creatures."

"OK, thanks," I said, heading away from the smell of his breath.

"You want to know how to keep moles out of your garden?" Reverend Leroy shouted.

I stopped in my tracks. "Yes." I looked at Ira and Grandpa, who were both grinning.

Reverend Leroy ignored them. "Mix up a spray of three parts castor oil to one part lye soap. Put 4 tablespoons of this in a gallon of water, and then soak the mole entrances and tunnels. They'll go away in a jiffy once they get a snoot full of that concoction."

"Really?"

Reverend Leroy's disgusted look told me I had gone too far. "Wouldn't you?"

I drew a circle in the dirt with the toe of my shoe.

"Hey, boy," Reverend Leroy said. "Did I ever tell you about the time I got struck by lightning?"

No doubt he lingered from the effect.

The auctioneer had started his rapid-fire talk to sell the first cow. Before he was done there would be fifty or more cows, horses, pigs, goats, sheep and a dozen or more chickens and turkeys auctioned. I loved the sound of his rapid-fire chant. It was like hearing a good song.

"Who'll give me fifty dollars for this fine yearling steer? Forty-five dollar bid, now fifty, will you give me fifty?

Dad didn't buy anything we had everything we needed for the time being. On the way home Dad asked, "What did Reverend Leroy have to say?"

I told him about his tips.

"Tell you about being struck by lightning?"

I nodded.

Dad chuckled. "The blast was actually from a stick of TNT. He was illegally dynamiting fish. After that, he quit making moonshine and got religion."

That didn't surprise me. I turned my attention to my pest control problem. My list looked good—everything was something I could find and make-work. I could hardly wait to start the projects. Ira came by that afternoon and helped me put up chicken wire. During the next week, I followed the rest of the advice I picked up at the sale barn. The garden had a nice yield and Mom canned plenty of vegetables for us, Grandma and Grandpa. At summer's end Dad said we had the fewest number of critters in our garden of any year he could remember.

Chapter 4

Gathering Eggs at the Chicken House

I walked out the back door of our farmhouse on a warm summer morning carrying a wooden basket lined with blue and white gingham. One of my jobs each day was collecting eggs and feeding the chickens.

The air was heavy with the sweet smell of new mown hay. A ray of sunlight streaked through the leaves of a sycamore tree that shaded the smokehouse where cut up parts of a hog I helped my grandfather butcher were stored. I blinked and looked away as I walked down the path toward the chicken house.

I opened the door and used a metal bucket to scoop corn from a wooden storage bin. I walked back outside and stood in the middle of a feeding frenzy as a dozen Rhode Island Red hens gathered around me, clucking and pecking the corn I tossed onto the ground. The rooster who was king of the flock sat on a wooden fence post crowing. It was as if he had gotten word from the big bird I hooked that ended up dinner I was not to be trusted.

Rhode Islands are big birds with dark red feathers. A rooster can weigh up to ten pounds, and the hens go as much as eight. The reason Dad bought that breed is each hen can be counted on to lay one egg every day, which was all we needed. Mom usually fried half dozen eggs for breakfast and used the rest for baking. Sometimes she would pickle a few along with some pigs' feet.

I helped Dad cut down an oak tree in the woods on our farm and he used the lumber to build a new chicken house to replace the old one that burned down after getting lightning struck. The old one was just a cobbled up affair but the new one was pretty fancy. It had a pitched roof. The north wall was shorter than the south wall. A half dozen windows on the taller wall gathered light and heat, which helped keep the flock laying eggs during winter. In a loft under the roof, we stored straw I used when I cleaned out the twelve chicken nests, which lined the wall from one end of the fifteen-foot-long building to the other.

I carefully placed the egg from each nest into my basket as I worked my way down the line of wooden boxes. I thought I heard a noise and stopped. On occasions I had encountered rabbits, possums, a skunk, mice and a rat that wandered into the shed seeking shelter. It must be the wind, I thought, as a gust rattled one of the windows. The distraction caused me to make a big mistake. Without looking first, I reached in the next nest and touched something that moved. The next thing I knew, a three-foot-long black snake slithered up my arm, fell onto the dirt floor and wriggled away over the top of my bare foot.

"Ahh! Ahh!" I screamed, ran out of the hen house and jumped up and down, shouting. "Snake! Snake!"

Dad rushed out of the house from the screened-in back porch. ""Did you get bit? What kind was it?"

Some of the snakes on the farm, like copperheads, were poisonous. I shook my head.

"I don't think so," I said.

"You know better than to reach into a nest without takin' a look first," Dad said.

I hung my head so he wouldn't see tears well in my eyes. "Hope I didn't break the eggs when I dropped the basket?"

"Come on, son. Let's go back in the hen house and see. We'll get the rest of the eggs." Dad put his arm around my shoulders, and we went inside. Only one egg was broken which Trouser ate. We gathered the rest and headed back to the house. All the hens and the rooster followed us through the barn lot.

The pattern of seeing things in my mind before they happened was starting to become more frequent. The day before I saw a dead black snake in front of our house that had been run over. I had seen copperheads, king snakes and a couple I didn't know what they were, but never a black snake until that day.

Chapter 5

Eating Poison Ivy

The summer I was six years old I was in the woods behind our house with my friend Tommy. He was one year older than me and always seemed to know more than I did. We were out looking for morel mushrooms; it was after a rain and the sun had peeked through the clouds, so Dad said we might find some. Dad knew everything when it came to dealing with the outdoors: when the trees and wildflowers would bloom, when the birds would have chicks, and about almost everything written about in the Farmer's Almanac. We ate a lot of morels mixed with scrambled eggs. Sautéed in garlic butter, the combination had a taste like eating raw corn, which I liked.

Along the way to mushrooms, we ran across a poison ivy vine growing up the side of an oak tree.

"I heard if you eat poison ivy you'll never get it again," Tommy said.

I grabbed a leaf and put it in my mouth. My tongue started to itch, my eyes watered and my throat clogged up, so I couldn't swallow.

We raced to the house, I told my mother what I had done and she put a teakettle of water on the stove so I could breathe in the steam. It was a miserable couple of days with blisters in my mouth. I was lucky to be alive, because poison ivy does the same to your insides as it does to your skin. I don't recommend it but I'll tell you what—I was never affected by poison ivy again.

When my grandpa heard about what I had done, being a man of few words, he said, "Poison Ivy is grown in the garden of hell."

"Tell you what, Son," Dad said. "Next time you want to do something stupid, hit yourself in the head with a hammer." Dad didn't talk rough often, but when he did you got the meaning.

Chapter 6

Mother's Stories

I used to sit at the kitchen table while my mother cooked. That's when she shared her stories. Most were centered on growing up in the Ozark Mountains. Fishing and camping with family and friends at Jacks Fork and Current Rivers which was a big source of entertainment during the summer. Come winter a lot of people play cards and board games like Monopoly. There was one trip where our family, neighbors, Grandpa and Grandma and dog Trouser all camped at the river for seven days. We hauled four bales of straw along, and spread it out on a gravel bar close to the water that's where we slept. Nine people and one dog under the stars lulled to sleep by the distant sound of a hoot owl and a whippoorwill.

One day while we were there mom was swimming in front of the campsite and she started to scream as she scrambled to get out of the water. A dead snake, cottonmouth no less, had drifted down the river and wrapped it's slithery body around Mom's neck. She told that story so many times she even told it to me twice and of course I was there.

Mom was a wonderful storyteller and had a great personality. She was good as gold but had a rowdy side when she was younger. Like the Halloween night she went with some kids to the cemetery and they made wailing sounds to scare people as they came past. The sheriff, Brian Jenkins for sure didn't take kindly to the kids turning over a couple outhouses, which some people call "privies." Stupid as it sound, that was a tradition on Halloween night.

What interested me most were stories she told about some of our relatives who lived in Germany, they suffered terribly during World

21

War II. She used to ship hard to find items like sugar, soap, coffee, clothing and shoes before the war broke out in 1939, then after it was over in 1946. She used to read some of the letters she received from my aunt and uncle out loud. Sometimes she would cry before making it to the end.

The first day mom got word the war was over and it was okay to send packages again she packed up half-dozen boxes of goods and when I went with her to the post office it seemed like her world had changed totally for the better from troubled times.

Mom loved to bake. She baked a lot of apple and pumpkin pies, cakes where mostly chocolate at my request, which I would eat hot out of the oven.

The big treat came on Sunday after church when Mom stirred up the mix for vanilla ice cream and I turned the crank on the wooden freezer. To top it off was warm, homemade chocolate syrup with walnuts sprinkled on top.

We harvested enough walnuts in the fall to fill half dozen gunnysacks. We dumped them in the road in front of our house. The green outer shells would be knocked off as people drove up and down the road. After hulling, we gathered the walnuts, sat at a table in the back yard, cracked them with a hammer and picked out the nutmeat.

There was no electricity in our neck of the woods until the early 1940s. Kerosene lamps provided light once the sun went down. When I close my eyes and think back to those simple carefree days, I can see the thick yellow flames dancing inside the glass mantles. The outlines of everyone in the room cast dark shadows on the walls. The smell of burning oil permeated the air. After the dishes were cleaned and put away Mom and Dad usually got out a deck of cards and played a few hands of Pitch, sometimes called High Low Jack or All Fours, before going to bed. Trouser and I curled up on the sofa with a blanket and drifted off to sleep. Next thing I knew it was morning. I had no memory of Dad carrying me to bed. My wakeup call was a rooster crowing from the barnyard. A Rhode Island Red Dad bought at the sale barn for 25 cents. The new bird looked just like the one I hooked and we ate.

I heard Don Roberts, one of the boys a year younger than me, ask Bill Brown who taught a class about farming if rooster was needed to get eggs?

"Nope, he said. "But there are a couple of other reasons to consider keeping a rooster around. A rooster helps protect the hens against intruders like snakes and other critters because they are bolder. They fertilize the eggs. While you don't need a rooster to get eggs, you do if you want to hatch your own chicks."

Chapter 7

Rendering a Hog at Grandpa's Farm

"Best not let your Grandpa tell scary stories before bedtime," Mom said as I hurried out the door.

"OK, Mom. I won't." I waved over my shoulder as I climbed on my bike and peddled down a gravel road toward Grandpa's cabin.

"Come in," Grandpa hollered when I walked up on the porch and opened the creaky wooden door. He was sitting in a rocking chair with his back to me stoking the fire. Brightly colored sparks danced up the chimney.

"How'd you know it was me?" I asked.

"I'm an old river rat," he grumbled. "Got eyes in the back of my head. Close the air hole."

I shut the door. The lock clicked. Something was wrong. Grandpa usually jumped up and hugged me at the door. A strong steamy odor, like a trace of vinegar, cut through the smell of wood smoke and tickled my nose. A yellow flame in a kerosene lamp on the kitchen table made the knotty pine walls look like the knots were moving.

I hung my coat on a nail and looked at the sparkling glass eyes in Grandpa's trophies. They seemed to watch me as I crossed the room. He'd had some of them almost fifty years. I slumped into a brown leather chair beside the stone fireplace and looked up at the stuffed deer head above the mantel. A ghost of the shiver I'd felt the day I touched the dead deer's cold wet nose came back to visit me.

"What time we getting up in the morning?" I asked.

Grandpa laid his pipe on a table beside the rocking chair and groaned. "Five o'clock sounds about right. Time I fix breakfast, time we get ourselves fed, it'll be daylight."

I figured even though Grandpa probably wanted to turn in early because butchering a hog was a hard day's work, he would still tell me a scary story first—the way he always did. Then I would sleep on the rollaway bed in his room. That way if I had a bad dream, he would be close.

Instead, he said, "You best sleep out here by the fire tonight. I'd just keep you awake tossing and turning."

"You won't bother me none, Grandpa." I looked at a bobcat hide nailed to the wall behind the couch.

Grandpa gave me a vacant stare as if he had not heard what I said. He looked around the room. "I've been thinking about getting rid of all these hides and mounts."

"What about the big buck?" I asked, pointing to the deer head with a ten-point rack.

"Him, too. Don't want nothing dead and gone around me anymore."

I pointed at the crow on top of the gun case in the corner of the room and grinned. "Blackie, too?"

"All of it," he snapped. "You want it? Take it."

25

I scooted my chair closer to the fireplace and watched Grandpa out of the corner of my eye as he rocked in his chair. It scared me that he was not his old self. "Is something wrong?"

He got up from the rocker and looked at me with pale, watery eyes. "Don't mean to scare you. It's just right now my mind is troubled. I'll be OK. Don't worry your cotton-top head about it none."

"OK." I looked away.

"I'm plumb tuckered out. Going to turn in early. You'll sleep better out here. You won't have to hear me snoring like a train."

I forced a smile. "Yeah, you're probably right. I'll read the book you gave me about storytelling. If I can't hear a story, I can read about how to tell one."

He patted my shoulder. "You're a good boy, lookin' after your old grandpa." He shuffled toward the bedroom. It was the first time I noticed how stooped over he had gotten. "If you get scared in the night, you can come sleep with me," he said as he disappeared into the darkness.

"I'll be OK, I think."

I tossed a cedar log on the fire and stared at the dancing flames. I turned a setscrew on the base of the kerosene lamp Grandpa had brought in from the kitchen and raised the wick so the flame burned brighter. I got up and walked around the room to look at the mounts and hides on the cabin walls. I wanted to assure myself once again that everything was dead, in case they chased me in a nightmare during the night.

Wrapping a wool blanket around my shoulders, I sat in Grandpa's rocker and stared at the fire until I drifted off to sleep. The next thing I knew, Grandpa was patting me on the arm.

"I've got breakfast ready," he said. He tossed a pine tree branch on the glowing bed of coals, and the dry needles burst into flame. "It's a crispy cool morning. Good day for butchering a hog."

"How long have you been awake?" I stood, stretched my arms over my head, and yawned.

"Hour or so, I guess. Went out and started a fire under the scalding vat. Takes awhile to get the water boiling."

I sat at the table. Grandpa had fixed my favorite breakfast, eggs and frog legs. I forked a pair of legs onto my plate, along with a scoop of scrambled eggs.

"You feeling better today?" I asked after I gnawed the last bit of meat off the bone.

Grandpa frowned. He looked at me through bushy white eyebrows. "Been sleeping uneasy."

I sopped up the last of the scrambled eggs on my plate with a piece of bread. "What's wrong?"

Grandpa washed down the last bite of sausage with a gulp of black coffee. He got up from the table and motioned for me to follow him out the door.

It was so cold I could see my breath when we left the cabin. The sun rising over the top of the barn cast a golden glow on the frost-covered ground as it shone through the red and yellow leaves on the maple trees. The *cock-a-doodle-doo* of a rooster sitting on a fence post broke the morning silence. I hoped more than anything it would be a good day for Grandpa.

Grandpa looked up at the clear blue sky and smiled. "Mother Nature's a good one isn't she?"

"Looks like everything's turned to gold," I said. A falling yellow leaf drifted in front of me as we walked through the gate by the chicken house and out into the feedlot where we would be butchering the hog.

Grandpa leaned the .22 rifle against the fence and walked over to the black metal scalding vat where red and yellow flames lapped up the sides. A wisp of steam rising from the bubbling, boiling water signaled that it was time to kill the hog. The smell of wood smoke hung in the air and sparkling frost covered the ground. We walked over to a long wooden table where a pulley was tied to a tree limb. A rope dangled. After Grandpa shot the hog, we would use the contraption to lift the carcass into the air, swing it over and lower it into the boiling water to loosen the bristles.

Grandpa picked up a knife with a deer horn handle and dragged the blade back and forth across a sharpening stone. He feathered the edge with his thumb to check for sharpness and laid it on the table in front of me. "Knife needs to be razor sharp to scrape off the hair."

I frowned. "I know, Grandpa. I've helped butcher before. Remember?"

He nodded. "I know you have. It's time to shoot the hog."

He walked across the barn lot and stopped in front of the fat sow. He shouldered the rifle the way he always had in the past, only this time, instead of pulling the trigger, Grandpa lowered the rifle and circled the hog as if he might ask her for a dance.

I walked up beside him. "What's the matter?"

He shouldered the rifle again as if he were going shoot the hog, and I backed up. He stood there so long that the sow waddled off toward the corner of the fence.

Grandpa lowered the rifle, walked over to the bench under the oak tree by the rendering press and sat.

"What's the matter, Grandpa?"

He lowered his head and stared at the ground. "Don't tell another soul what I'm about to say. People will think I'm crazy. They don't need much excuse to put an old man like me away."

"I don't think you're crazy, Grandpa. I love you. You're the smartest person I know."

He smiled. "Been having a terrible dream." He pulled a bandana from the hip pocket of his bib overalls and wiped his mouth.

"It'll be OK, Grandpa. I have scary dreams too."

He leaned back against the trunk of to an oak tree. "In my dream, someone outside my bedroom window calls my name. I walk outside the house and follow the sound of footsteps to the river's edge."

I swallowed a lump in my throat.

28

"I'm surrounded by wild animals. They're all staring at me with shiny glass eyes."

"It's just a dream. That's all."

Grandpa laid his shaky hand on my arm. "Every night I walk farther out into water."

"What does it mean?"

He shook his head and handed me the rifle. "Take it. I can't kill the hog. You have to shoot her if she's meat on the table."

The only things I'd ever shot were a squirrel and a couple of rabbits. Something was different about shooting an animal I helped raise.

"Do we for sure need the meat, Grandpa?"

"Be a long winter without any sausage. No ham for Christmas dinner." He patted me on the shoulder and gave me a way out of my misery. "We can get your dad. He'll shoot her. He gets half of the meat, you know."

I wanted to say OK. The words were on the tip of my tongue. Instead, I walked over to the hog and shouldered the rifle. Like Grandpa, I stood there and could not pull the trigger.

"It's OK," Grandpa said. "Let's get your Dad."

Tommy had shot a hog, and sure as the world, he would hear I chickened out. I moved in closer to face my fear, laid my cheek on the gunstock, and picked a spot between the sow's eyes where a little brown clot of mud was stuck to some white hair. I took a deep breath, let it out slowly and squeezed the trigger. Instead of the hog going down after the sharp crack of the .22 shell, the beast just stood there and stared at me. I had completely missed. My stomach churned.

Grandpa hurried over and grabbed the rifle. He ejected the empty cartridge, bolted in another shell and handed it back. "Best go on with your job." He patted me on the back. "A man needs to finish what he starts."

He walked away, leaving me with my hands trembling.

I moved in close and shouldered the rifle again. I took a slow, deep breath. I aimed at the mud spot again and squeezed the trigger. The crack of the exploding shell echoed loudly. The hog looked at me and blinked as if nothing had happened. I felt faint, and my legs went weak. I could not shoot again. The old sow staggered to the right, back to the left, slumped to the ground and rolled over on her side.

"Good shot, son," Grandpa said, as he ran his fingers back through thinning white hair. "Wasn't your fault you missed the first time. She moved her head as you pulled the trigger. That happened to me once when I was your age."

He walked over and looked into my eyes. "You finished what you started. That makes me proud. Let's swing her into the scalding vat and get on with the butchering."

After the day was done and we had a winter's supply of meat in the smoke house, I went to bed that night thinking how lucky I was to have a Grandpa who knew stuff and showed me things.

The other thing I was happy about was at breakfast he told me I would do good things because I had a unique mind. I knew he himself was a constant thinker. Like me, Grandpa thought about things then they happen. He could tell the details about coming weather a couple days in advance.

Chapter 8

Ozark Mountains Outhouse "privy"

Grandpa was on his way to the outhouse one stormy night when a bolt of lightning struck the tin roof and the little white building burned down. I know it's true because grandma told the story to everyone who would listen and she was a God fearin' woman who never told a lie and would walk out of the room if a lie were being told.

The outhouse structure, sometimes called a 'privy', which everybody in the Ozarks had at least one of before indoor plumbing and electricity came along.

During the course of my youth and the times I frequented the little white building located a few hundred feet away from our farmhouse, I had some unusual experiences. Even though a few were traumatic and troublesome at the time, they seem funny now.

When I was about seven years old I sneaked a .22 rifle cartridge out of my Dad's hunting coat, took a wooden match from a box in the kitchen and headed for the outhouse to create a fireworks display. I laid the shell on the toilet seat, struck the match and when the flame touched the metal casing there was a loud explosion.

Moments later I shoved open the heavy oak door, stumbled outside and ran toward my mother who was working in the garden. My final words before I fell onto the ground were "I'm blind." What happened was when I looked down at my thumb and saw the brass shell casing sticking out of the nail that had been blown there by the explosion and saw blood dripping onto my bare leg, I fainted. When my mother poured water on my face I came around and realized I could still see even though things looked blurry. Dad pulled the brass casing from my thumb with a pair of pliers and I fainted again.

When I was about ten years old during a bitter cold winter day I slammed the wooden door shut and the hook on the outside fell into the latch, I was trapped until Grandpa came to use the privy. He almost had a heart attack when he opened the door and I knocked him down as I rushed outside.

There were spiders and snakes in the summer who liked to share the outhouse with us humans and once an a opossum was waiting inside because the door had blown shut when he was seeking shelter on a winter's day. As slow as those critters are generally, he didn't waste any time scrambling out the door.

Of all things, the building had a tin roof so when it was very hot in the summer like the temperature hovering around 100 degrees on the outside, it would be at least 120 degrees inside the outhouse. There would of course be the smell and the flies and the occasional mouse running across the floor to escape when I opened the door. Needless to say visits were postponed then short as possible.

Here's a little history and additional information about the outhouse that might come in handy if you're ever in a situation where you must use one even though you probably won't be, but you just never know.

The basic design for the outdoor toilet hasn't changed for hundreds of years. It's just a shack sitting over a pit in the ground. The inside has a bench with holes cut into it. Generally there's a bucket of lime and a scoopful is poured in before you leave.

Until recently as the 1930s most every family had at least one sometimes two or more outhouses. Then they began to disappear with the advent of indoor plumbing. During the Great Depression, the Works Progress Administration (WPA) built a least a couple million or more pit privies.

I heard more jokes about outhouses than anything I can remember. Strange as it might seem outhouses were the center of attention Halloween night. Mostly, rowdy boys would tip them over and on occasion Tookie Brooks, a classmate who was always getting in trouble fell into the hole during the process, a dangerous and smelly experience. Most people kept a close eye on their privies during Halloween and would even fire a shotgun up in the air if they saw kids sneak around who seemed up to no good.

Because of having a large family, Grandpa had two outhouses side by side. One had a crescent moon cut into the door and the other a sunburst. The reason for the symbols is they would provide light and ventilation, and the moon, or Luna, is an ancient symbol for women, while a sunburst stood for men. These symbols started being used back at a time when very few people knew how to read.

Once a new Sears, Roebuck and Company catalogue arrived the old version found a place in the outhouse to be used as toilet paper.

Chapter 9

Grandpa's Hay Barn

Grandpa built a barn in 1902 that was admired by many. One day a cattle buyer from St. Louis came to our place to buy a couple of steers. He stood in the feedlot admiring the sixty-foot tall structure the way someone might look at a work of art. "Wouldn't it be nice if people aged as gracefully and remained so strong," he said

Born Dead on a Winter's Night

Dad, dog Trouser, me and a couple of chickens followed the fella inside so he could get a closer look. We had fed all the hay mowed during the summer to our cattle and horses, except for a couple of cooing pigeons sitting on a rafter at the top and a spider scampering up a spun web, the barn was empty. The fella looked around at the open space and said; "I feel a sense of peace and connection with the earth standing here. This barn would make a great church."

I waved as the buyer drove away in his shiny new 1950 Chevy pickup truck pulling a trailer with a couple of steers inside that I helped raise. One I bottle-fed after the mother died. A bit of a sadness seeing my furry friends go away, I brought myself back to thinking about how lucky I was to have a place where I could daydream. My routine would be to lie on a pile of loose hay and travel places in my mind that I had read about in books. It could be everything from a cowboy or an engineer, to a writer or an artist. On special days when storm clouds rolled in that brought the splatter of rain to the tin roof, I became the captain of a paddle wheel boat floating down the Mississippi River with Mark Twain headed for New Orleans. He would smoke his pipe and tell stories about Tom and Huck that would be scary one minute and funny the next.

In the summer the sweet herbal smell of new mown hay would tickle my nose. In the fall a tangy whiff of apples picked from the orchard and stored in wooden crates blended with the sharp smell of sap from freshly cut cordwood.

I loved the sights and sounds in the barn. The whinny of a horse in one of the stalls, the cluck of a chicken scratching the dirt floor searching for a last kernel of corn, the gray and white barn cat, Sly, stalking an ever-present mouse. I would watch her move forward slowly, low to the ground. She stopped, ever so often so she would not frighten the little gray creature away. Suddenly as a gust of wind, she would rush forward and catch her prey.

On a clear night, when moonlight shined through the open doors, I sensed the presence of others who had been in the barn before me, especially Grandpa who had cherished the structure so dearly. Other times, the spirits of neighbors, relatives and craftsman who helped raise the barn many years earlier. All of them had gone to rest.

On many occasions during my time at the barn my intuitive gift would appear. I would think about something and it would happen. If I thought about a deer within a reasonable time one would appear. Clair cognizance is a curse and blessing, when you talk to others especially if you are a kid, generally people think something is wrong.

The barn was a sanctuary from the time I could walk until I moved away from the farm when I was seventeen.

When Grandpa built the barn he told everyone at the raising the structure would be strong enough to last at least one hundred years. It has survived tornados; hail storms, lightning and high winds. There's a possibility it will be standing two hundred years or more. Anyone who knew Grandpa would not have expected anything less. Floors and siding of the structure stayed strong as the day the oak trees to build it were cut off the ridge. Every brace was rugged hand hewed four-by-six foot beams.

Grandpa said people came from miles around to help with the raising. Some workers framed the walls, fitted the support braces and nailed the structure together. The women brought fried chicken, loaves of fresh baked bread and potato salad to be served with all the lemonade people could drink. Kids played croquet, skipped rope, fished the pond and took turns cranking the handle of the ice cream freezer. Lots of laughter and dancing after the walls were raised.

Good will is generated when an entire community helps build a barn. It brings people closer together. The owner is beholden to everyone for the help.

Every year since the summer the barn was raised, Grandpa filled it with loose hay to feed a herd of Hereford beef cattle and a Holstein milk cow. After Grandfather's death, my Dad took over the farm and continued to fill the barn with hay. However, things were not the same as in the old days because of an invention called the hay baler.

Grandma's would spread the word when a dance was going to be held at the barn. During good weather, most Saturday nights, my job was to sweep the dirt floor and knock down cobwebs to get ready for the shindig. Grandpa built a stage under the hayloft where a fiddler and a couple of guitar strummers played bluegrass music until wee hours in the morning and people would square dance. By the time I was twelve I took over as the caller. I loved every minute of the attention. Sometimes I would get paid as much as a dollar.

One Saturday night when the barn dance was in full swing, Tookie Brooks said he was going to ride the hayfork, over the heads of the dancers.

The idea was so stupid I did not even answer him until he got close to my ear and assured me everything would be okay. I shook my head and looked away. Tookie's middle name was trouble; he looked for it on a regular basis and had no trouble finding it often.

The hayfork was made out of metal, looked like an over-sized set of ice tongs and was used primarily to pick up loose hay from a wagon and lift it into the barn with an attached rope, which would be pulled to open the tongs at a location where hay was to be dropped. However, Tookie and I used it for a fun ride as well, which was dangerous and not for the faint of heart.

To get where we could grab hold of the tongs to start the ride, we first had to climb a thirty-foot ladder that was attached to the wall of the barn up to the second story hayloft. From there we climbed another thirty-foot ladder and crawled onto a small platform. When it was time to take a ride, we grabbed the hayfork by the tongs and shoved off. As the pulley traveled along a rail our speed increased. By the time we were fifteen feet away from the other end of the barn, about seventy feet from where we started, we would sale through the air like a bird. At that point we kicked our feet out level with our chests, let go of the hook, and fell twenty feet or so landing flat onto our backs in a cushion of soft hay. The most important part of the operation was to let go in time so as not to smash into the wall.

I pulled Tookie to one side so he could hear me over the hoedown music. "You're the only one who will think it's funny. If you fall you might kill somebody."

I could tell by the way his eyes glazed over that my warning went in one ear and out the other.

"People will see you climb the ladder," I said. "Your mom will be mad. Your allowance will be gone."

"I'll wait until a new dance starts. They won't see me climbing. Everyone will be looking at their partner."

At the start of the next song, Tookie eased his way along the wall to the front door of the barn until he reached the ladder and climbed to the second story. I looked around and it seemed nobody had noticed. From the hayloft he climbed the second ladder another thirty feet and crawled out onto the platform. I looked around when he waved. I could not believe nary a soul had seen him climb to the top.

When the last fiddle tune ended, Tookie let out a yell that sounded like a bobcat caught in a briar patch. He grabbed the hayfork tongs, shoved off the platform and headed toward the other end of the barn like a circus performer. A half dozen pigeons flushed from the gable as the pulley traveled along the rail. By the time Tookie was close to the other end, a cloud of brown and white pigeon feathers floated through the air.

"Let loose," I yelled. Either he did not hear me, his hands were frozen to the tongs, or he thought he was tougher than the oak barn boards he was about to confront.

Tookie had the attention of everyone at the barn dance.

No doubt most of the kids had never seen anyone knocked unconscious before because a couple screamed and turned away. Some surely thought he was dead. In a couple of minutes, Tookie got his wind back and was on his feet. His only injuries were a bloody nose and dislocated finger swollen to the size of a large carrot.

His Mother walked up beside me and shook her head. She was so used to Tookie's antics that one more stupid trick did not seem to be a big deal. Being the good mom she was, Mrs. Riley put her arm around his shoulders and helped him walk to a bench where she poured him a glass of water.

Once Tookie recovered from one injury, he was ready to try something else daring.

A couple of weeks after the dance we were in the barn again hanging out when Tookie announced he had a cigarette and asked if I wanted to smoke it.

He had taken a Lucky Strike from his dad's pack and it was in his pocket.

I told him I did not want to smoke the cigarette. I had already gone through the experience of trying to be a big shot a few months earlier, got sick and threw up the first time I breathed in a puff of smoke.

Besides that, Dad caught me sneaking a smoke, and gave me "what for" in no uncertain terms, which included a whack on the butt with a willow tree branch. So for the time being, I was determined to leave well enough alone.

"I don't want to. You can if you want. I remember the last time you smoked when you cut down a grapevine and fired it up. Your tongue was sore as a boil for two days."

"Okay fine, I'll do it myself." Tookie pulled the Lucky out of his pocket and paraded around with his head held high and the cigarette dangling from the corner of his lips.

"I've got to go back to the house soon," I said. "I hope you don't get sick. If you do you'll have to stay in the barn."

"Bull. I'm too tough. You know that well as I do." There was a loud pop as he exploded the head of a wooden match on the metal strap button of his overalls. He put the flame to the end of the

39

cigarette and inhaled deeply as if he were trying to suck cobwebs off the rafters. The smoke barely got into his lungs before he went into a violent coughing fit and his eyes filled with tears.

"That didn't take long," I said, holding back a laugh, as I did feel sorry for him. Mainly I was glad it wasn't me. I grabbed the Lucky from his hand and spit on the fiery tip to put it out. I did not like the idea he played with fire in Grandpa's barn, it was too dangerous. Seconds Later, Tookie heaved up his lunch.

"You look pale," I said. "Are you okay?" I smiled to myself, hoping he would think twice before he tried it again.

Tookie wiped his slobbery mouth on the sleeve of his blue cotton work shirt and in a weak and whiny voice he mumbled, "I'm quittin'. Never smokin' again an gettin' sick."

"You never was tough as me," I said, giving him a poke on the shoulder with my fist. "Take some deep breaths. You can't go to the house lookin' like you've seen a ghost, my mom will know what you've been doin' for sure."

After half dozen deep breaths I grabbed Tookie by the hand, led him over to the stock trough and splashed water in his face. He started to look better.

I gave him a pat on the back.

"Feelin' better too." He slowly walked around in a circle and wiped the tears from his eyes with the back of his hand.

"Want to go up and ride the hay hook?" I asked. "Maybe you'll do a better job this time".

"Don't be stupid," he said, not thinking much of my joke.

"Feelin' good enough to head to the house?" I asked. "We can walk slow." He nodded his head and we headed out the door.

When we got there Mom had peach cobbler waiting for us on the kitchen table. It was fresh out of the oven. Steam rose off of the crust and a sweet cinnamon smell filled the air. I thought there might be trouble brewing when she grabbed Tookie by the arm, looked into his eyes and said, "You need to get out in the sun more, Tookie. You're a bit peaked."

Fifty years after I moved away from the farm to the city I returned for a visit. I was interested to see how the barn was holding up more than anything else. It looked almost the same. As I stood in the feedlot and stared at the big gray oak building with a silver tin roof, I remembered how I helped Grandpa and Dad work in the field. We loaded loose hay onto a wagon with pitchforks, worked in the blazing hot sun and hauled it to the barn. We hoisted the hay with a hay hook, pulled it inside, and dumped it in specific spots to fill the barn evenly.

After I checked out the house and corncrib I walked around the pond where I used to catch catfish, bass and bluegill using worms from Mom's garden using a corncob bobber and a cane pole. My eyes filled with tears from a rush of nostalgia. From the driveway I took one last look and remembered the time Tookie rode the hay hook at the square dance crown and I laughed.

Chapter 10

A Belgium Draft Horse Named Clyde

Belgian Draft Horses are the most popular of all draft breeds in the United States. They are one of the oldest and most powerful horses, bred for industrial work, farm work and have the ability to pull tremendous amounts of weight.

The draft horse my grandfather owned whose name was Clyde was 17 hands (68 in./170 cm) tall and weighed over 2,000 pounds (900 kg). I spent a lot of time working in the field with that big brown beauty and loved Clyde so much.

I tossed and turned in a sweat soaked bed. It seemed like I'd only slept a couple of hours when Dad opened the bedroom door and clapped his hands. "Up an' at 'em". We've got a day's work to do."

I picked up a corner of the bed sheet and wiped sweat from my eyes. It had been a hot, sticky night, and I woke every time the grandfather clock in the living room chimed each hour on the hour. If my mom's dad hadn't given her the clock, I would have gotten out of bed and destroyed the chimer.

I looked out the window at the blazing orange fireball rising over the top of the hay barn. The promise of another day hovering around one hundred degrees glared back at me.

"Breakfast is ready," Mom yelled from the kitchen. "Get yourself in here. Your Dad wants hay hauled in today. It's supposed to rain."

I hopped to the floor, grabbed a pair of bib overalls from a cane bottom chair and pulled them on. I slipped into a long-sleeve blue denim work shirt and wiggled my feet into my high-top work shoes. Long sleeves were the order of the day when putting up hay to keep itchy alfalfa seeds off sweat soaked skin.

I smiled to myself as I headed down the stairs only one more workday in the hay field, and then it was Fourth of July. I had saved my money and bought five dollar's worth of fireworks—mostly M-80s, which were powerful enough to blow a tin can into the air the height of a sycamore tree.

"You be careful with those firecrackers," Mom said as I walked into the kitchen, where she had a plate of biscuits and gravy and a glass of milk.

"You know I will." I sat down and forked a gravy-covered biscuit into my mouth.

"Your Dad's finished breakfast. He's outside hitching Clyde to the wagon. You should finish hayin' today. Then you can start diggin' sprouts."

I hated the thought of digging spouts out of the ground so badly I played like I didn't hear what she said. If you just cut them down they would just grow back the next year.

Clyde was our big Belgian draft horse that did many different jobs around the farm. Sometimes I rode him along the river. He was a good swimmer and loved the water. I felt bad that he had to work so hard and figured he hated the heat as much as I did.

We were into our third day of work to put up fifty acres of alfalfa. Clyde had pulled the sickle-mower to cut the hay. We left it to lie in the field drying in the sun to prevent spontaneous combustion which would burn down the barn, Dad worked Clyde in the woods hauling out logs from a dozen oak trees he had cut down to sell to the sawmill.

When the hay was dry, Clyde pulled a 10-foot-wide dump rake with a set of long, curved steel tongs mounted on a frame set between two wheels. The rake swept the hay into rows. Today, Clyde would pull the wagon while we used a pitchfork to toss hay onto a flatbed and we would haul it to the barn. There, we'd use the hayfork to lift it inside the barn. The one Tookie and I used to ride and he rode over the top of the square dancers.

After I gobbled down breakfast and gave Mom a peck on the cheek, I met Dad in the barn lot. Then we headed for the hay field.

With the sun blazing, Dad on one side of the wagon, and me on the other, Clyde started down the first hay row, with only a "Giddy up!" from Dad. The old horse slowly walked across the field and when Dad said, "Whoa!" Clyde stopped.

At first people did not believe Clyde would do such a thing as pull the wagon without a driver. But after folks like Preacher Roberts and Mr. Simpson, the banker, saw it first-hand; nobody doubted Clyde's talent anymore.

Once we'd lifted the second load of hay off the wagon into the barn, the sun blazed high noon. We stopped for lunch. I led Clyde to a water trough under the shade of a big oak tree, scooped up a bucketful of water, splashed some on Clyde's neck, and rubbed the white froth off his skin. I glanced over my shoulder to make sure nobody was looking and got up close to Clyde's big old ears. "I love you, Clyde. I wish you didn't have to work in the hot sun."

He turned his head and nudged me when I looked into his big, brown eyes. I know it was all in my mind, but I had no doubt he understood what I had said.

We sat at a long harvest table to a heap of fried chicken on a big white platter, along with a bowl of potato salad and a pitcher of lemonade. Grandma Mary had baked a brown-crusted apple pie with gooey cinnamon sauce oozing from the top. After lunch it was off to one of the shade trees in the yard for a thirty-minute snooze. Then we headed back to the field knowing the workday was half done.

At the end of the day, the hay was out of the field and in the barn enough to feed twenty head of Hereford cattle, a milk cow, and a couple of goats for the winter. I led Clyde out into the pond and splashed cool water on his back. He turned his head toward me and rubbed his soft, pink nose on my neck.

Starting day after Fourth of July, the next hot job would be digging sprouts with a broad head axe. It was amazing how many tree saplings grew back year-to-year. If we didn't keep the crop chopped, they would take over and cover much needed grazing land.

What kept me going on the sprouts was the fact Clyde got a little time off. There was neither man nor beast that deserved it more. With the work done, my mind filled with thoughts of the Fourth of July and blowin' stuff up with my powerful M-80s.

Chapter 11

Good Thing There Was Only One Beer Joint in Town

I was sitting in the River's Edge pool hall and got a lump in my throat that usually signaled trouble. The door flew open and slammed against the wall. A rush of cold winter air introduced the Roberts brothers, Bill and Bobby. They stumbled into the pool hall in a violent embrace. Bill, the older and bigger of the two, had a headlock on his little brother who was groaning. Bill's teeth were clenched on his younger brother's right ear.

"Holy smokes! Who let those two rowdy character's in here?" Dan Riley, the town marshal, shouted as he jumped up out of his rocking chair. A dozen older men huddled around a wood stove in the middle of the room. The two brothers had been kicked out of the Up Town beer joint across town for fighting. They carried their ruckus to the pool hall, a gathering spot for locals on Saturday nights. The brothers were regulars who came into town every weekend from their cabin on the Current River. With the exception of store bought beer they lived off the land.

The other half of the building housed a two-lane bowling alley. Once I turned ten, only a year away, I would be old enough to be a pinsetter. It was a fast-paced noisy job clearing fallen pins and returning bowling balls to players. On a busy night a pinsetter could make as much as three dollars.

I was sitting in a chair by the front window watching Dad and Uncle Clyde shoot pool. I had the perfect view when Bill gnawed through the gristle of his brother's ear, and then spit the chunk of raw meat on the floor. It looked like a piece of chewed up popcorn, only a little darker in color. At that point, with blood dripping onto the collar of his denim shirt, little brother Bobby made a bold threat that would have scared me half to death. "Remember: I know where you sleep."

Dan rushed up front and grabbed the brothers by their arms and back out the door they went. Everyone moved to the front to watch as Dan ushered the rowdy two off to jail in the town square. I can only imagine the misery of being cooped up in a jail cell with a drunken brother who bit off part of my ear. Both were wearing bib overalls and long johns. Not much protection considering the jail cell had no heat and on that day the temperature was in the low 30's.

Plain as day, I still see the piece of earlobe lying on the dark oil-stained floor and the look of pain on Bobby's face. No doubt the brothers were destined to run amuck.

A couple weeks later their pickup truck ran off the steep road on Jacks Fork River hill and both were killed. There was always activity that spelled trouble at the beer joint. The occasional shooting was mostly due to drunken fights.

Dad said, "Good thing there is only one beer joint in town. We can't afford to lose any more citizens."

Chapter 12

First Day of School

It's easy to remember the names of classmates when there are only thirteen kids. For that matter, it's not difficult to remember the names of most people in town when there are fewer than one hundred residents. My first day of school at Summersville Elementary I had a life-altering experience that stayed with me from age six to the present day. A blonde girl with a laugh and look that had the power to gather a crowd was standing beside the aluminum slide with a half dozen other fidgeting kids.

"Have you talked with her before?" I asked Tommy who was sitting on the swing. He and I had gone on a couple rabbit hunting trips together with our fathers. We carried BB guns since we were to young too be trusted with shotguns or rifles. Tommy fished in our pond with me during the summer and we caught half dozen catfish.

Tommy shook his head. "I don't know her but she's getting a lot of attention."

I had seen her before but we never talked. She lived in town, and I lived on a farm in the outskirts. Her family owned the Chevrolet car dealership. They were Baptist, and we went to the Methodist Church.

Something about the girl caused me to think differently. I wanted her to like me but had no idea how I could make that happen. When you're that young, plotting for the long haul is not a strong trait. My second day at school I had a brilliant idea. I picked up discarded chewing gum and cigarette tin foil wrappers. I molded my treasure, which grew bigger and bigger until it was the size of a baseball. When the object of my quest was alone in the cloakroom I gave her the shiny prize. She seemed lost for words as she stared at the ball, then back at me, finally she laughed. It was obvious Marlyn liked it.

"Are you sweet on the girl you gave the ball of tin foil to?" Tommy asked. I nodded and at the same time, I had a feeling something might happen that would change our lives forever.

That moment in 1946 was the start of our lifelong relationship, which would result in the birth of two daughters, four grandchildren and ownership of a half dozen dogs over the years. Through trials and tribulations, long-term relationships are one thing I can recommend wholeheartedly. If nothing else works to get a female's attention, try a ball of tin foil. It's a proven success.

Chapter 13

Living Off the Land

"Get your sleepy time bones out of bed!" Mom yelled up the stairs. "Breakfast is on the table."

Year round we were up at daybreak to eat then do chores. The aroma of Mom's cooking drifted though my bedroom door and stirred me around. A typical morning spread included crusted brown biscuits stacked next to a gray stone crock filled with thick dark sausage gravy, hard fried eggs with crispy brown edges, a tub of butter and jar of honey in the center of the table, one on each side a pitcher of milk. Mom always cooked enough to share with my dog Trouser; he had a bowl by the cast iron cook stove. He lay at my feet until I called his name, then he jumped up and hurried to eat his people food.

Mom canned vegetables we didn't eat and stored them in mason jars in the cellar for winter food. Lined up on shelves along the walls it was like an art display: red tomatoes, green pickles and cucumbers, purple beets, yellow corn and golden honey from a bee hive in a field of clover.

I hated going into the damp, dark cellar to get food for Mom. Even when I didn't see anything, my imagination would take over and I could feel spiders crawling on me. It got better when I got older, but still, the cellar was one of my most unfavorable places. Every step the flame in the kerosene lantern flickered and created shadows on the musty walls. It was like being in a dungeon.

Going into the smoke house to get ham, brisket, ribs, rabbits, fish or deer meat was much better. There were never spiders, flies or snakes because the smoke order kept them away.

Born Dead on a Winter's Night

My routine to start the day was always the same. I slipped into my blue jeans and a denim work shirt, wiggled my feet into a pair of moccasins made from deer hide that Aunt Maude gave me for my birthday. Thick brown leather, handmade by some skilled person in a Native American tribe. On the box it said, Navajo. She bought them from Sears, Roebuck & Company, a mail order catalog that had everything a person needed to get along. I was proud of those moccasins since most other boys wore clunky-looking brogan work shoes that weighed at least one pound each.

I wore my mocs in the woods while carrying a bow and arrow Dad made from Osage orange, a tree that grew in our fencerow. It is one of the toughest woods on the planet. During the course of my trips, I killed half dozen rabbits, a couple of squirrels and a ground hog all of which we ate. I also shot an arrow into a red fox, which was already dead, but I didn't tell anyone.

Dad worked at the sawmill part time and had access to different kinds of wood. He made our kitchen table out of pine and a coffee table walnut. A couple of tables made of oak for Grandpa and Grandma sat on each end of a couch in their living room.

"Now you've finished building the kitchen table, I'll put away the red and white checkered oilcloth. The table is to beautiful too cover up," Mom said.

One of my favorite things Dad made was a rabbit trap: a box about 2 feet long and 10 inches wide. A door attached to a wooden trigger that slid up and down in the trap, which was baited with a carrot or lettuce. When a creature went inside and moved the bait, the door closed. In addition to rabbits, we caught a couple of black snakes and squirrels, one raccoon and, my least favorite, a skunk. One of my jobs was to check the trap each morning. I learned early on not to stand in front of the door when I opened it. The first day I checked the trap when I got on my knees and looked inside, a huge rat ran out and snapped at my nose.

Speaking of critters, Tommy and I went to Grandpa's house, looking to be entertained.

"Tell us a story," I said.

He settled into a big wooden rocking chair on the front porch and rocked a while in silence.

We sat quietly watching him for at least a full minute before he spoke.

Normally Grandpa smiled when he started a story. This time I saw nothing that looked like a happy face.

"Has either of you boys ever skinned a possum?" he asked.

I shook my head. The only thing I had skinned was squirrels and rabbits. And as best, I knew Tommy's only experience came from plucking the feathers off a dead chicken or two. After we confirmed there was no possum skinning experience between the two of us, Grandpa told his tale.

"I brought in an ol' sow possum and a muskrat this mornin' when I ran the trap line, and one of the most God-awful, strangest things happened. Something I feel terrible about, but there's nothing I can do to remedy it now except to tell you boys so you don't ever let the same thing happen to you."

Tommy frowned at me.

I figured the way Grandpa hesitated, the story would pack a double-barreled wallop, and with the next thing he said, there was no doubt that's what was coming our way.

"You boys know I'm a kind hearted man and I don't kill things unless there's a reason."

Tommy and I nodded.

"I run my trap line every day no matter how bad the weather. I don't want to leave an animal caught in a steel trap to suffer. That's the code for a good trapper. I only trap for hides to sell at the feed store for extra money. Lord knows we can always use a little more of that, and we eat every raccoon. I feed the possum, beaver, and muskrat carcasses to the hogs, so there's no waste. That's the kind of thing has to happen when you're livin' off the land."

I wasn't sure I wanted to hear what awful thing had happened. I knew Grandpa's daily routine. He got up at daylight, grabbed the .22 rifle leaned in the corner by the front door, picked up a gunny sack he kept on the front porch, and went to check half dozen traps he'd set along the river. He would be home in an hour or so for breakfast. In a good year, he trapped a dozen raccoons and possums, eight or ten muskrats, and a couple of beavers.

The price he got for hides depended on the number of animals from year to year. Weather and food supply were the main factors determining the wildlife population. In a slow year grandpa made about $125, and during the best year I heard him tell about, he made almost $250. He had to spend money for .22 rifle shells, a new trap now and then, and new pairs of leather gloves and boots every couple year. It was a lean business that was a lot of work and hardship in exchange for what a trapper had left at the end of winter.

"I'm telling you boys this story because I want you to hear it from me and not some kid at school that blows up the details out of proportion. Since your grandma had a couple of friends visiting who saw the whole damned thing take place, no doubt the story has already spread from here to hell and gone."

"Go on, Grandpa."

"This mornin' it was cold and snowy when I ran the trap line. I slipped and fell twice before I got to the last trap, and when I did, a beady-eyed old sow possum whirled around and hissed me to a stop. I jumped back, raised my rifle, and shot her between the eyes. I walked up and poked her with the rifle barrel to make sure she was dead before I threw her in the gunnysack with a muskrat I got out of my first trap. The problem with possums is they really can live up to their reputation of playing possum. I've known a lot of trappers who thought one was dead, but it turned out that they were wrong."

"They must be hard to kill," Tommy said.

Grandpa took a deep breath and nodded. "When I got home, and started to clean my kill, I skinned the muskrat first. Then dragged the possum out of the sack and poked her in the belly a couple of times with the point of my knife, just to make sure she was a goner. I skinned her out and threw the carcass over the fence for the hogs. As I stretched the hide over a board, I heard a ruckus in the barn lot and looked around. What I saw should only happen in a dream so it can be erased from a person's mind."

Here, Grandpa paused and shook his head. "The naked old sow was walking toward the woods a flock of chickens in hot pursuit. I feel terrible that the poor thing would have to go through winter without a warm coat."

Tommy and I looked at one another with big eyes no doubt Grandpa's story would be a lasting memory.

I set a few traps and made extra money selling hides when I was in high school and was always extra careful when it came to skinning possums.

Some of the things we did to survive might seem cruel, but living off the land was a challenge. However, the price paid had many rewards. So many if I tried to list them I might run out of paper. Simple things, like squirting a stream of milk into the mouth of our yellow barn cat Bob. I always smiled as the cat rubbed up against my leg, licking his whiskers to get the last drops of milk. His actions seemed to say, "You're nice to me, and I want to be nice to you."

Chapter 14

Low Tech Entertainment, High Tech Fun

There was excitement when Mom said, "Hook up the radio, I'm poppin' corn. Dad carried what was called a farm radio, which was housed in a wooden case the size of a milk crate outside of the house. He raised the hood on our dark green 1939 Chevrolet pickup truck and set the box on top of the engine. The radio was designed to run, not off of household electricity, but a six-volt battery so it needed to be close to make the connection. In the late 1930's and early 1940's, before TV and FM became widespread, the radio was designed to receive AM stations and shortwave, a powerful band that could even get a signal from as far away as China. Strange as it may seem, I heard voices of a language I did not understand seconds before Dad turned the radio on first time. Imagine every one's surprise the first time he turned it on.

Most Saturday nights during the summer, unless there was a barn dance at our place or one of the neighbors, we invited Grandpa, Grandma, and Aunt Maude over to listen to broadcasts like *The Shadow, Grand Ole Opry, and fireside chats by President Franklin Roosevelt during World War II.*

We enjoyed a warm summer evening sitting in the front yard under the stars eating popcorn and drinking sassafras tea. My dog Trouser lay in front of me knowing I would drop a few kernels. With the glow of lightning bugs flashing, I envisioned the bellowing bullfrog at the pond beckoned me to have frog legs to eat with eggs for breakfast. It would simply be a matter of getting the gig and a flashlight off the back porch. Go to the pond and follow the deep throated bellowing sound as I creep quietly around the pond bank until I saw a couple of glowing yellow eyes. Once I gigged the kicking green frog I would scrap it off the gig prongs into a gunnysack. Then head home to the cleaning board where I cut off the creatures head, gut it with my hunting knife and skinned it using a pair of pliers. Mom always rolled everything she fried in cornmeal and made sure the meat was crispy brown.

When Dad said, "*The Shadow* should be coming on next, I moved closer to Mom, since it was scary. I suspected the adults were a little bothered by the suspense as well, but nobody said a word.

We never traveled farther from home than the Jacks Fork or Current Rivers, which were only ten miles away one direction or the other. Trouser and I rode in the back of the pickup, which today would be frowned on as unsafe. All I know to say about that is I'm still alive.

The summer breeze as we traveled along a dirt road was filled with the smell of honey suckle and wild roses. Thirty minutes after Dad pulled out of the driveway we'd be swimming in one of the cool, clear, spring-fed rivers. Most times we saw nary a soul, even if we were there all day. It was as if Mother Nature created the outdoor paradise just for us. Years later I read an article in *Life Magazine* where the author proclaimed the Jacks Fork River one of the most scenic fishing and float streams in the world.

I said we never travelled. Actually, we made trips to Springfield, Missouri about one hundred miles away to see relatives a couple of times. When we got back home, Mom said, "Not sure why we want to travel; we already live in paradise."

Chapter 15

Riding the Bull Calf

Tommy lived on a farm about five miles outside of town with his dad, mother, and a sister named Lucy. Everyone said she was a tomboy and I discovered early on they had no idea how wild she really was. In addition to livestock and chickens, they had a dozen coonhounds and a couple of cats. Tommy I did a lot of stuff together, fished, hunted, camped, and rode calves in local area rodeos. Rodeos were fun because even if you got bucked off, which we did a lot, there would be memorable applause.

I was at their house one afternoon when Tommy's dad backed up to the loading chute at the barnyard, and down the ramp ran a yearling calf weighing about a thousand pounds. After getting a drink of water and saying goodbye to the missus he was off to the sale barn. He had a dozen turkeys and a hog to be auctioned off. As he pulled out of the gate he yelled at Tommy, "Don't be ridin' that calf!"

Soon as the calf walked into the barn we hopped over the rail fence, walked across the feedlot and into the darkness of a two-story hay barn.

Here I will admit to doing something that seemed okay at the time but not for the long haul. Sometimes boy's who are only twelve years old have a distorted view of what's right and what's wrong. Fun and the way the wind is blowing is a big factor.

Tommy talked me into riding the calf by saying it would be good practice for a local rodeo coming up in a couple of weeks.

We cornered the calf and got a rope around the middle so I would have something to hold on too. Once I settled onto the bull's back, he headed for an open door like a shot out of a cannon. The problem came when the bull calf jumped and my head hit the top of the door, the quick, sharp pain made me think I may have been struck by lightning. Lucky me, it had rained the night before and a soft pile of cow manure provided a cushion for my landing. I looked up at Tommy who seemed to have a halo above his head from the effect of my fall and said, "What are we going to tell your Dad?"

Tommy shook his head. "If you live, I'll say I hit you in the head with a baseball bat… accidently."

I lived. By the time Tommy's dad came home, except for a sharp pain in the front of my head and a red spot—which I covered with my baseball cap. I was almost back to normal, except that night I dreamed I was run over by a calf at the rodeo.

Chapter 16

The Headless Man

I was obviously destined to be a slow learner when it came to avoiding self-inflicted pain.

My horse trouble started with a picture of a Shetland pony I saw on a sack of feed at the MFA Market. All black except it had four white stocking feet. He looked like a slice of heaven on four hoofs.

I showed Dad the picture. "I'd be on my best behavior forever if I had a Shetland pony."

Dad laughed. "That's a big time promise."

A couple weeks went by and one day Dad showed up with a golden brown Shetland pony he bought at the sale barn for forty dollars. The sight of the little horse took my breath away. I had visions of rides through the woods and along the river. Problem being, the pony was a wild one, not only did he chase cow's, he also chased turkey's who took shelter in a big oak tree by the corncrib. I had never seen the flock fly until that day. Normally they enjoyed a laid-back life, pecking at grain and gobbling grasshoppers. I named the pony, Bad Boy.

Dad finally got a rope on the pony and led him into a small barn we mainly used for cows when they were about to give birth. Since there was no birthing going on, it was Bad Boy's home for the time being. His rowdiness was one of the biggest let downs in my life.

I had heard there was a way to communicate with horses by getting close to their ears and talking softly. On a regular bases, things I thought about actually happened, so naturally, I thought I might be able to calm the new pony down.

When I told Dad my plan he said, "You can do anything you set your mind to."

I tossed and turned in a sweat-soaked bed thinking of what would happen the next morning. At daylight I dashed out the door and headed for the barn where I hoped something magical would be waiting.

When I opened the door, standing in front of me bathed in a ray of sunlight was my golden beauty, Bad Boy who I hoped would become one of my best friends. He stared at me and I got the feeling he thought some of his troubles were actually my fault. The possibility of us becoming friends made me lose control of my reasoning.

I walked inside the barn and rubbed my newfound friend on the neck. He rubbed my arm with his wet, black nose. That seemed like a breakthrough so I climbed on the pony's back and leaned over to whisper in his ear.

What came next changed my life. Bad Boy jumped high in the air and sailed through the door. My head hit the top of the doorframe, knocking me onto the ground, unconscious and into a pile of horse manure. For a couple of minutes, history repeated itself only this time with a different animal. The pony ran off to the backside of the field.

"My oh my, what happened to you?" Mom asked when I stumbled in for breakfast.

With a hangdog look, a red knot on my forehead and a feeling of being sad and sorry I said, "I may never get on a horse again."

Chapter 17

The Good

Simple things, being outdoors cutting and splitting wood to heat our house and my mother's cook stove. Working in the garden, planting seeds, pulling weeds, harvesting crops, picking strawberries off the vine which I ate as I worked. Hunting, fishing, and gigging suckers on spring-fed rivers. Working with Clyde our Belgium workhorse cutting and putting up shocks of loose hay in the barn before the advent of the hay bailer. Going to the mill with Dad to render sugar cane to make molasses, butchering a hog for meat to hang in the smoke house, milking cows, slopping hogs, feeding chickens and gathering eggs, my Dad taught me all those things and more. Memories of shooting marbles with boyhood friends, Tookie Brooks, my best friend Tommy, Iver Riley, Bobby Bell and Buck Maggard, whose Dad sold him a canoe rental business at Acers Ferry on Current River in Missouri for one dollar on his birthday. I played softball, baseball, basketball, and a girl with blonde hair I called Tin Foil Girl who seemed to like me more as time went on. I figured that was true because instead of a short hello and goodbye, she would stop and talk. Say things like, "What are you doing during the weekend and you must have been out in the sun a lot you have a nice tan."

These are some of the things I remember, no doubt there were a lot more.

Chapter 18

Gigging Suckers on an Ozark River

I smiled at Dad as I climbed into the cab of his pickup truck and closed the door. I was twelve years old and never floated the river at night during the winter. I was excited to be on my first sucker-gigging trip. Gigging is using a spear with three metal prongs to take fish or frogs rather than to catch them on a hook or by hand. Suckers are bottom-feeding fish that are tasty as any fish I have eaten when taken from Ozark Mountain's spring rivers.

Mom walked out the front door of our white two-story farmhouse and waved as Dad pulled away from the driveway onto a gravel road.

"You all be careful," she yelled.

I waved and yelled back, "We'll see you at the cook site."

Dad shifted into second gear and we headed toward the river access ramp at Buck Hollow. The setting sun filled the woods with shadows, a breeze rustled the leaves the temperature had fallen ten degrees in the past half hour. We drove past tall pine trees and stately sycamores that lined the bank along the creek bottom. The white bark on the sycamores made them look like ghosts in the moonlight.

"You okay about goin' tonight?" Dad asked.

"Sure," I said.

"You seem nervous."

"Not sure I can stab a sucker." I had some doubt about being able to handle a 14-foot gig pole covered with ice and gigging a sucker swimming along the river bottom in water ten or twelve feet deep.

"Why not?" Dad asked.

"They swim fast." I did not want to float into the cook site without gigging even one fish.

"You'll do fine. We'll gig enough suckers to feed everybody."

"How many do we need?" I pointed up ahead as a buck deer with a ten-point rack crossed the road. A doe, and a fawn with white spots followed.

Dad shifted into low gear as we started down a steep rocky hill about half a mile from the river. "A dozen redhorse and a couple of hogsuckers will be enough to feed the crowd."

"Hope I can hit one."

"You'll do fine, Son. Just slide the pole into the water and follow along until the gig is a foot in front of the suckers nose. Then shove the pole hard and stab the sucker in the head. Make sure it's a sucker, not a bass. It's not legal to gig game fish."

"I know a sucker from a bass," I tried not to feel insulted about knowing one species from another.

"It's easy to get them mixed up. That's all I'm sayin'. Grab the gloves from under the seat. It will be gig pole freezin' cold tonight, the kind that settles in your bones."

Dad was right about it getting cold; I felt a chill in the air as soon as the sun went down. I put the deerskin gloves in my coat pocket and wished I had worn a second pair of socks to keep my feet warm.

I hopped out of the pickup to give Dad directions while he backed up to unload our green 16-foot wooden jon boat. I caught the toe of my shoe on a tree root and fell, slapping the back fender with my hand on my way down.

Dad heard the commotion and yelled, "Are you hurt?"

"I'm okay." I looked down to see if my knee was bleeding. I couldn't tell for sure in the fading light. I groaned, "Pull on back."

"Don't let me get too close, "Dad eased the pickup toward the river's edge. "Don't want to get stuck in the loose gravel."

"Okay. That's good," I yelled as I rubbed my knee and felt a tear in my jeans the size of a half dollar.

Dad got out of the pickup. We pulled the boat from the truck bed and slid it into the water. Loaded a couple of 14-foot poles with three-prong gigs attached, a carbide light, and a thermos of boiled coffee. Dad climbed back in the cab and parked the pickup under a cottonwood.

"Why'd you bring the pistol?" I asked when I noticed Dad had strapped on a 38-caliber revolver he used when he went coon hunting.

"Never know what you might run into on the river at night," Dad said as he picked up the carbide lamp.

"How long have those been around?" I asked as Dad fiddled with a valve to get the light ready.

"Long time. Miners started using them many years ago. They're dependable lights."

"How does it work?" I asked.

Born Dead on a Winter's Night

Dad pointed at the lamps reservoir. "Water stored here drips into the carbide chamber and makes acetylene gas. The gas passes through this tube and onto the tip. Simple operation."

Dad struck the head of a wooden kitchen match on the button of his bib overalls, touched the flame to the gas spewing from the carbide tip, and a circle of white light the size of a living room appeared instantly.

"Carbide light covers a wide area as you can see," Dad said. "Years ago those who gigged burned jack pine knots. They'd put a wagon wheel in the middle of the boat and wedge a burning knot into the center, turn the boat sideways and float downstream. A pine knot didn't put out as much light as carbide, but those old boys still gigged lots of fish."

Dad hung the carbide lamp on a hook attached to a waist-high railing above the gigging platform, and the carbide light lit up the river bottom like it was daylight. When we climbed into the boat, Dad grabbed a pole, turned the three-pronged metal gig upward and used the blunt end to push us away from the bank.

"What do suckers eat?" I asked.

"Aquatic insects, mayflies, and cicadae are mainly. That's why you don't catch 'em on a hook using bait the way you do most other fish. We're on our way." Dad poled the boat into the middle of the river and the current carried us downstream.

Hoot. Hoot. Hoot.

I looked around when I heard the call of an owl and saw a shadowy image of the big bird as it flew across the river. I looked up in the early nighttime sky and saw a few stars. Soon there would be so many it would look like a river of sparkling diamonds.

"What time will the moon come up?" I asked.

"Should rise above the bluff top in an hour or so. The moon's full tonight so it will make a lot of light. Look at that beauty." Dad pointed at a snow-white icicle hanging from a rock ledge that was 10 feet long.

I picked up the other gig and climbed onto the platform. I stood beside Dad as we floated silently downstream, looking for suckers that would swim over a river bottom covered with white, gray, and reddish gravel and green moss. I imagined we were a couple of cavemen on the hunt for fish to feed our family.

"There's a big one," I said as a fish three feet long swam into the glow of our carbide light then quickly disappeared into the darkness.

"Gar," Dad said. "They're rough fish. It's okay to gig 'em if you want too."

"I know it was a gar, too long and skinny to be anything else. How far is it to the cook site?" I asked.

"About five miles. We'll be there around ten or so. Somethin' botherin' you, Son?" Dad asked. Like I said earlier, you seem nervous. I know you had a bad experience where you almost drown last year when the river was running high.

I nodded my head and looked up at the stars.

Dad put his hand on my shoulder. "The bad feeling will pass." He picked up a rope and tied one end around my right ankle. The other end he tied around the front seat. I laughed. It did make me feel safer knowing I could be pulled into the boat.

"How long have people been gigging?" I asked as I stared at a sunfish beside a sunken log, slowly fanning his tail in the current. A smallmouth bass that weighed three pounds or more swam into the circle of light. Just as quickly the fish darted away into the darkness and headed toward a beaver dam where a spring branch ran into the river.

"People have gigged for centuries. That's how Lewis and Clark got a lot of fish on their expedition. Cavemen used spearheads made of rock or bones. They tied 'em to the end of long poles with sinew and use them to stab fish."

"What's sinew?"

"It's the long, strong tendon that supports an animal's backbone. It's like fiber. They'd strip it out and use it like thread."

A fish with reddish fins appeared in the light. "There's a sucker," I said.

"You saw him first. He's all yours, son."

"Go ahead. I'll get the next one." I wanted to see how the gig master did it first. Dad slid the three-prong gig into the water, moved the pole until it was a foot in front of the sucker, and hurled the gig into the fish. The pole quivered as the sucker twisted back and forth and tried to get free. Dad reached down and picked the pole up from the icy water, looked at me, and smiled.

"Wow," I said as he brought the sucker around to the side, lifted it into the boat and used the seat in the back to dislodge the fish from the prongs. I patted him on the back, and he smiled.

"One down and a dozen to go," Dad said as the redhorse sucker flopped around in the bottom of the boat. "Next one's yours." He grabbed the thermos, unscrewed the top and poured himself a steaming cup of coffee.

We floated a half-mile downstream through another riffle and a still hole of water where we saw one of the biggest walleyes I had ever seen but nary another sucker.

"There's your sucker," Dad said as he pointed to my left where a big redhorse worked his way upstream.

I slid my pole into the water and stalked the fish until the gig seemed to be in the right place. Then I shoved the pole at the sucker as hard as I could. I missed and the fish swam away. I looked at Dad and shook my head.

My fear of us pulling into the cook site without me having gigged a fish came back again in full force. I believe some of the things I worried about were caused by premonitions, feeling something was going to happen that did much of the time. In this case I didn't want to be teased by my friend Tommy.

"Wasn't your fault," Dad said. "The fish got spooked and darted away. It's happened to me a lot."

Before I could say anything a hogsucker swam into the light. The brown and white spotted fish was moving slowly along the river bottom heading straight for me. I slid the pole into the water, positioned the gig just right and thrust it toward the fish. The next thing I saw was the gig pole wiggling back and forth and prongs sticking through the sucker's head. I swung the pole around and scraped the fish off the gig using the back seat.

Dad smiled. I smiled. The full moon was rising above the top of the limestone bluff that towered over the river, and when I looked up at the heavens, a shooting star streaked across the sky.

During the next couple of hours, we boated a dozen nice-sized fish, ten redhorse and two hogsuckers. As we floated past Buck Hollow cave, we heard a high-pitched scream. Dad unsnapped the safety strap on his holster.

"Probably a bobcat," Dad said as we floated past. "Female cats are like women; they'll only put up with so much from a mate."

"Hey!" Tommy yelled and waved as we rounded the bend a couple hundred yards upstream from the cook site. Dad and I were standing side-by-side on the gigging platform, which was lit up like the Milky Way on a star filled sky. I waved and felt proud. "Did ya get any suckers?"

"More than you'll be able to eat," I yelled and Dad laughed.

A loud scraping sound filled the air when we pulled the jon boat onto the gravel bar at the cook site where half dozen people stood around a blazing fire warming their backsides. A couple of Dad's friends walked down to the river, loaded the fish into a gunny sack and hauled them to a spot set up with a cleaning board. Beside it lay a couple of knives to scale and score suckers for the fish fry.

"You boys gig enough to feed this hungry bunch?" Mom asked as she stoked the fire burning under a cast-iron kettle, half full of bubbling pork lard. Flames lapped up the sides. She was in charge of the sucker fryin' operation; nobody any better that was for sure.

Dad walked up to Mom and gave here a hug. He looked at me and smiled. "We sure did. My helper gigged his fair share."

"No reason why not," Mom said proudly. "Not nothing my boy can't do when he sets his mind to it."

"I've got the potatoes sliced and ready to fry," Mary, a friend of Mom's, said as she sat a white crock on the table.

"How long 'til the suckers are cleaned?" Mom asked. When the report came back frying could take place in ten minutes, Mary dumped the bowl of spuds into the boiling lard and a cloud of steam shot up into the air.

A fella named Jim, who owned the river front where we were having they sucker fry, carried a couple of brown paper bags that contained a cornmeal, salt, and pepper mixture which was used to coat the fish before they were cooked down to the river.

Tommy and I followed him to the place a couple of fella's were hard at work, scaling, then scoring the suckers by making deep cuts about one eighth of an inch apart for the entire length of the fillets. That allowed the boiling hot pig lard to cook the needle sharp sucker bones so they would be soft enough to eat. After cleaning, the meat was dropped into Jim's brown paper bags, which he shook up and down with the vigor of a couple dogs after the same bone.

I carried one paper bag heavy with filets and Tommy carried the other, which we sat on a table close to the fire so they could be deep-fried. After Mom scooped the potatoes out of the kettle with a ladle and piled them onto a platter. She dropped the sucker slabs into the bubbling hot lard and a loud crackling sound filled the air.

Everyone had a plate ready for the feast when Mom scooped up the deep-fried sucker meat and piled it on a big white platter beside the potatoes. A treat after the tasty meal was roasted marshmallows. I was not paying attention when one of the men lifted the kettle of smoking hot grease off the cooking fire and set it behind a log.

I wandered over and sat down on the log and put my hand on the damp, slick surface. Then my hand slipped off into the kettle of grease that moments earlier had turned the sucker meat crispy brown.

"Yeow!" When I felt the heat and knew what I'd done. I jumped up and ran to the river, figuring the ice cold water would give me some relief.

"What's the matter?" Mom yelled as Dad hurried to the water's edge with the carbide light. When he held it out in front of him, I looked down at my hand and saw the skin was gone, burned away by the blazing hot grease. "Look," I yelled as I held up my hand for Dad to see then put it back in the cold water to ease the pain. My hand was nothing but white bone.

Everyone gathered around watch me to cry and shiver. Dad waded out into the water for a closer look and discovered what I thought was nothing but bone, was actually pig lard coated on my hand and fingers. I had saved myself from a severe burn by jerking my hand out of the kettle and plunging it into the freezing water.

Dad covered my hand with wet leaves, wrapped it in a gunnysack and we headed home. As long as I live, what I will remember most about my first sucker-gigging trip was not that I gigged some fish, not that I was cold to the bone floating down the river, not that I almost burned my hand off, but that suckers are the most delicious tasting fish ever to swim in a spring-fed Ozark Mountains river. I also knew that most people would never eat even one in their entire lives.

Chapter 19

The Bad

A few months later, when I was thirteen years old, my father, Ray Love, died as a result of complications from a car accident. He was driving down the Jacks Fork River hill swerved to miss a deer and ran into a deep ravine. It was late at night and he was not found until the next morning. It would be impossible to describe the trauma of losing a parent when I was so young. People told me something went wrong at the hospital. Someone said medical personnel let the cylinder run dry while Dad was in an oxygen tent. Sixty-five years ago many hospitals were under staffed and personnel who where responsible for taking care of patients with breathing problems were not well trained. I stood at the gravesite as the casket was lowered into the ground. The cables squeaked as the shiny black tomb disappeared.

People came up to me and said, "We're sorry for your loss. You're the man of the house now. You must be strong." I was so full of grief that their words sounded hollow. Living on the edge of darkness, I felt nothing but despair. No hope that my life would be the same again. If I felt so sad and lonely, what about my mother? What could I say that would be meaningful? How would we survive? My father was my best friend, a strong man with a heart of gold who was only thirty-five years old when his life was taken away.

One day I walked into a cave at the Jacks Fork River, a place where Dad and I used to swim, and yelled, "I hate you God for what you did to my mother and me." The echo made the message seem more powerful, like God could hear me better and feel bad for what he'd done. Maybe he would perform a miracle and bring my father back to life. I heard about miracles over and over at church with my mother. No doubt it could be done.

Even though my mother was as strong as any human could be, she was haunted by the death of my father. The fact that he was taken away so young made it worse.

"Do what you love and live life to the fullest," my father used to say. He was a farmer and loved every day of his life. I rode with him on the tractor as we plowed fields to plant grain and cut hay. Dad loved to grow things for man and beast to eat. He taught me how to catch and clean fish, hunt rabbits and squirrels and take care of farm animals and chickens. "Always tell the truth or learn the hard way."

What would I do now?

Chapter 20

More Bad News

Six months after I saw a bald eagle in a dream. At this point a daily occurrence of premonitions had become routine. Uncle Clyde drowned in the Jacks Fork River, a stream that seemed so peaceful it could only bless one's soul. Clyde was swimming close to a limestone bluff and got tangled in a pile of sunken brush. I was upstream catching crawdads for fish bait when I heard people scream and start to cry. By the time I reached our campsite, Clyde was face down, drifting in the current.

Above my head a bald eagle soared, hovered over Clyde's body then disappeared into a cloudless blue sky. I had never seen an eagle on the river before nor had anyone else in our group. I thought the massive bird's flapping wings were taking Clyde's spirit to the next world. When I told my mother she said, "Your uncle has gone to meet your father to make sure neither of them gets lost."

My dad and uncle would do anything to help people in need, especially older folks who lived in our community of a couple hundred souls. I remember sadness day after day, wondering if I would ever feel whole again. Time does heal and the best memories come to light as the sadness fades away.

Chapter 21

Growing Up in the Ozark Mountains

People who grew up in the Ozark Mountains are among the most superstitious group in American history. Their intuitions generally involved things like

• A red sunrise is a sign of rain.

• If a rooster crows near the back door, company is coming.

• Ghostly visions of the Ozarkians are often believed to be beloved family members coming back from the dead to offer help or comfort.

There were hundreds, often used in daily conversation. The superstitions are passed down from one generation to the next. They have endured for all these years because, lurking in the next deep hollow, hovering over a blue-hazed ridge or coming around the bend, there is enough magic to keep the legends alive. The beliefs are constantly reinforced; the way past generations thought about the world they lived in gives a clearer picture of their lives, perhaps better than any other accounts can. Folklore is the people themselves talking.

Outsiders never understood why those of us who lived in the Ozark Mountains believed so strongly in folklore, assuming we were not wise to the ways of the world. Truth be known, we treasured what was passed on to us it was the reason we were deliberately unprogressive. We enjoyed our lives. We smiled and waved when city folks drove up in new cars wearing fancy clothes, thinking how we were poor country folks. Nothing was further from the truth. Even though we wore bib overalls and went barefoot much of the time, we had a sensitivity beyond anything the average city slicker could imagine.

Once, my grandpa was talking to an outsider who came to our part of the county to fish. That's what the man said, anyway, but we all knew better. What he really wanted was to pick up moonshine whisky that old man Hartman cooked in his still up on Buzzard Ridge. He sold it by the gallon jug for a dollar.

The visitor from the city was telling Grandpa how the Depression had been so bad that city folks were standing in bread lines. Grandpa listened, then nodded and waved when the city fella climbed into his car and drove away.

Grandpa turned to my dad. "What kind of trouble was that city fella talkin' about anyway?"

During the Depression we had no less than before hard times hit the rest of the country. We grew our own vegetables, hunted game, and lived off the bounty from a nearby river. We had little need for money we were self-sufficient.

Chapter 22

Relief from Grief

The summer after my father and uncle died, I got some relief from living in the shadow of sorrow. My mother agreed to cook at my cousins' fishing camp Cardinal Acres, downstream only one mile from where Clyde drowned. For the first couple weeks after we moved to camp, I dreamed of Clyde floating in the water. Sometimes the eagle that had appeared that day swooped down and carried him away.

The camp was a wonderful outdoor experience. Swimming in the cool, clear, spring-fed water, diving off limestone bluffs, fishing and guiding tourists on float trips down the river made me feel grown up.

Born Dead on a Winter's Night

One of my most memorable trips was the day I guided a couple of fellas from St. Louis ten miles downstream to a pick up point at Bunker Hill Resort. When we rounded a bend a dozen black buzzards were feasting on a dead cow. They had been at it for a while as the belly of the beast was open and the guts where gone. When we got within a couple hundred feet of the activity, the birds took flight. I grabbed my Stevens Crack Shot 22 rifle and fired at one that was overhead. The city fellas sat in amazement as the bullet made a loud thud when it hit one of the wing feathers.

My shot caused the buzzard to regurgitate a large amount of red and white liquid the texture of buttermilk, which splattered the faces and chests of my paying customers. They had given me $5.00 to paddle a jon boat during a 10-hour float. The smell of buzzard puke, which the birds use to escape their enemies, smells a lot like rotten eggs, only worse. It was so bad Bob, the tall fella in the front, gagged twice.

"Was there a reason why you shot at the buzzard in the first place?" Bob asked, when he was finally able to talk.

"Not a good one," I said as humble sounding as I could muster. "I won't do it again today."

What saved me was both Bob and his friend Phil caught more fish than ever in their life because of my guide skills and, by the end of the float, they only smelled half as bad. They were nice enough not to tell cousin Vern what happened.

Ironically, our take out access at Bunker Hill was the place my mother and I would live the next summer while she cooked for guest. I could do the same outdoor jobs I did at Cardinal Acres, plus call square dances. Mother and I had to leave Cardinal Acres because my cousin decided his girlfriend would be doing the job my mother had done.

Soon after the federal government declared public domain on all of the property along the Jacks Fork and Current River's to create the Ozark Scenic River Way. Vern and other landowners fought the authority for almost one year, but in the end they lost. Vern was heartbroken that his paradise had been taken away, as were others who had property along the river. They were paid fair market value but where else could they go to replace what had been a piece of paradise?

Chapter 23

Cotton Mouth Water Moccasin

I'm going to get my stories about snake encounters out of the way so I can quit being scared. All of them are about cottonmouth water moccasins, North America's only venomous water snake. The creatures have a distinctive blocky, triangular head and a thick body. They pack enough poison in their large jowls to kill a human. If you make the mistake of hitting one with a rock, like I did, you'd better be ready to run, because they will attack when threatened. The snake can detect minute differences in temperatures so it can accurately strike the source of heat.

Zip your tent if you're camping. Be alert when fishing or hiking anywhere in the southeastern region of the United States. The name "cottonmouth" comes from the white coloration inside of the snake's mouth.

Snake experience #1

While living at Cardinal Acres Resort in the Ozark Mountains during the summer of 1953, I got up early one morning to swim in the river. I stood on the gravelly bar, warmed by the sun rising above a limestone bluff. It could not have been a more beautiful day; the kind you get once in a while when you think nothing could possibly go wrong.

When I waded into the water, I heard something upstream. Out of a driftwood pile appeared a cottonmouth the size of a man's arm, head raised high, tongue flicking in and out as he sensed the air to see if there was danger or food nearby. Obviously upset because I invaded his domain, the snake swam toward me. I had seen a couple of cottonmouths in the river before but none so close. The big brown reptile stopped when he got within ten feet, opened his mouth and dropped his fangs. When I saw the white cotton lining, I knew I was in trouble and might even be dead soon. It was as if the warning cry of a blue jay perched on a tree limb across the river was a signal for the snake to strike.

I jumped backward when the snake struck; his fangs scraped the calf of my leg. My heart was beating so hard I could feel it pulsing in my throat as I scrambled down the gravel bar. I imagined the snake sinking his fangs into me when I slipped on the loose gravel and fell to the ground, but to my intense relief, when I looked back, he slithered back into the water. Lucky me I got no poison in my leg, just a red mark and a dose of adrenalin that almost made me pass out. I went back to camp, got some matches and burned the driftwood pile. I never saw another cottonmouth in my swimming hole. However, it was not my last snake encounter that summer.

Snake experience #2

A couple months after the first cottonmouth encounter in my swimming hole, cousin Vern and I floated downstream a couple hundred yards from Cardinal Acres to gig bullfrogs in a slough, a pool of water off the main river channel. It was a pitch-black night, a whip-poor-will cried its familiar call, and an owl's deep sounding hoot, hoot, hoot filled the air. I silently paddled the jon boat in between a cover of lily pads. Cousin Vern gigged the first bullfrog that was resting on top of a big green leaf, and passed it back to me. I pulled it off the prongs and put it into a gunnysack. We went deeper into the slough and got half dozen more. The farther we went, the bigger the knot in my stomach grew. We had entered cottonmouth heaven.

When it was time to leave, I turned the boat around and dug the paddle deep into the water, wanting to get back to the main part of the river as fast as possible. Suddenly, all hell broke loose behind me. I shined a light and saw a cottonmouth had attached itself to the gunny. It took a few seconds for him to realize he had struck at the sack and gotten his fangs were tangled up in the burlap bag, obviously stuck. One of a cottonmouths favorite food is a frog. The fear I had the day I was attacked by the snake in my swimming hole came rushing back.

"What can I do?" I yelled.

"Beat him off with the paddle," Vern shouted. "Don't let him get in the boat."

I stood up to hit the snake with a paddle and almost turned the boat over. With the second swat I knocked the snake loose. I sat down and we paddled like maniacs. I was still shaking by the time we got back to camp. After we cleaned the frogs and Vern's wife fried them with scrambled eggs, I vowed never again to go back to that hole of backwater even during daylight. I didn't say anything but wondered if the snake might have dumped poison into one of the frogs and I might die during the night.

Snake Experience #3

I was a grown man in 2001 when I had my third snake encounter. My friend Mike and I planned a fishing trip on the upper Jacks Fork River, a remote 10-mile stretch of spring-fed water in the Ozark Mountains. During dog days of summer getting a boat downstream required dragging it over slick, mossy rocks at every ripple. Aside from being labor intensive, you would fall down a lot so we came up with a better plan.

What bothered me more than low water was, since there had been no humans around for a month or so, cottonmouth snakes would have moved into the area in significant numbers. Also, August, when we would be floating, was prime breeding time, mama snakes would be delivering up to twenty babies, each one about 10 inches long. The young are also dangerous. That was a little bit bothersome since our plan was to sleep out under the stars.

What we did so we could get down stream with the least amount of effort was buy a couple of inflatable float tubes called Fish Cats that were designed in the shape of a horseshoe with an open front for easy entry. Made of rugged space-age material, the tubes would slide over rocks easily, float in only 6 inches of water, weighed less than ten pounds and had comfortable padded seats. To move forward we would kick our legs back and forth, the flippers attached to our feet would propel us through a dozen long, deep holes we would encounter along the way. When we were not in the tubes floating we would wade in shallow water along gravel bars.

During the five-hour trip from Kansas City to the river, Mike and I talked about everything from the speed of a dragonfly to the best bait to use to catch the most fish. We had fished together for years and knew each other's moves. I liked to fish for sure, but with Mike, it was an obsession.

Born Dead on a Winter's Night

On our way down a steep hill that led to the river, a big buck deer leaped from an embankment and disappeared into a growth of oak tree saplings. This got our spirit of adventure stirred up. We stopped at a low water bridge where the north and south branches of the Jacks Fork River ran together, a place called Forks of the Creek. Hello outdoor world, goodbye civilization.

A wisp of fog rose from the clear spring fed water. Sunlight made the surface sparkle as if it were covered with flecks of gold. Mike stopped the SUV on a gravel bar and we unloaded our gear, which consisted of bare necessities: which included a couple of fast action, ultra-light G. W. Loomis rods and Shimano spinning reels spooled with 4-lb test line. Our lure boxes had a simple selection, a couple of crank bait crawdads, baby Jitterbugs, Zara Spook top water lures, a half dozen hooks with an equal number of split shot sinkers and a couple of Hildebrandt spinner brown wooly worm combinations.

Since we would be on the river for three days, we could take our time and fish around root wads, sunken boulders, and rock ledges for goggle-eye and catch smallmouth bass in the fast moving ripples. If we were unable to catch fish on artificial, we would use live bait picked up along the river bank, worms and crickets that hid under logs, small frogs that lived in the foliage along the river's edge. Grasshoppers, my favorite river bait, were plentiful in August. One thing fish found especially hard to resist was crawdad tails with the shell peeled exposing the white meat.

Our store-bought food consisted of two jars of crunchy peanut butter, a squirt tube of honey, a pound of coffee and a loaf of bread. Fish cooked over an open fire would be our mainstay. We figured the worst case, if we did not catch any fish, which was unlikely, once the peanut butter was gone, we could eat the plentiful crawdad tails and squirrels, which I could kill with my 22 pistol. We could tie a couple of air mattresses to our Fish Cats to float our gear and use them to sleep on at night.

We planned to explore a couple of caves along the way and fill our canteens with spring water that ran from the mouth of the caverns into the river. Blindfish lived in the deep, cold pools of water back in the darkness. Our bait of choice to go after the illusive prey would be a worm threaded onto a small, trout-sized hook.

We parked the SUV under the shade of a sycamore tree where it would remain until my brother-in-law, who lived in the area, came by later and shuttled it to our take out point on Sunday. Pulling our Fish Cats and air mattresses behind us, we waded downstream toward Chimney Rock where we encountered the first deep hole of water. We sat down in the seats and floated through it in our inflatables.

Someone driving a rusted green Chevy pickup, missing a front hubcap, drove across the low water bridge upstream and stopped. A tall, thin fella, wearing a straw hat, a blue work shirt, and bib overalls, dropped off a couple of pups on the bridge and sped away from the river in a cloud of dust.

The two dogs, one black and one white, looked down the river at us and wagged their tails. I knew potential trouble was blowin' in the wind. Little did I know how unsettling the adventure would become.

Mike yelled at me up the river, "What's the deal on those dogs?"

"Somebody dropped 'em off at the bridge. Didn't want 'em I guess."

"For sure we don't want 'em. They'll scare away the fish." Mike made another cast and hooked a smallmouth bass that tail-walked across the surface of the water. It would be a nightmare to contend with a couple of pups if they followed us downstream along ten miles of rough terrain and rocky overgrown banks and sometimes they would have to get into the river and swim a long distance. Not to mention the possibility of them getting bit by a Cottonmouth water moccasins ruled that lonely stretch of river and did not take kindly to intruders.

"What kind of dogs are they?" Mike asked.

"Maybe Labrador mix," I said.

The pups ran across the bridge, jumped onto the riverbank and headed down stream toward us, barking. I waved my hands in the air and yelled at them to stop when they were fifty yards away. They paid me no mind, so I picked up a rock and threw it in their direction. It splashed in front of them, but they kept coming. I felt bad about what I did next but I had to keep them out of harm's way.

"What are you doing?" Mike yelled.

I pulled the 22-caliber revolver that belonged to my grandfather from a holster in my fishing vest. I carried it on the river to protect myself from snakes, and to kill squirrels when I needed food. I shouted again but the pups kept coming.

"You're not going to shoot them are you?" Mike yelled.

I pointed the 22 out to the side of them 25 feet and squeezed the trigger. When a spray of droplets splashed up the pups ran into the brush alongside the river and disappeared.

"They wouldn't go back. I had no choice." I holstered the revolver and walked downriver.

Mike stood there shaking his head.

"Hey, Mike! The pups couldn't make it down river without getting hurt. I had to scare them off, I think we're rid of them now."

We waded downstream and as we rounded the bend, looming in the middle of the river was Chimney Rock, a 60-foot tall limestone structure the size of a grain silo shaped like the chimney of a house. It was shrouded with hanging poison ivy vines whose leaves had turned red with the coming of fall; the top was cloaked in a misty gray fog. The night before, I had a dream that my grandfather and I were floating the same stretch of river sixty years earlier when I was 12 years old. I cast a red and white Lazy Ike lure behind a big boulder and caught a 4-pound smallmouth bass. I was happy I caught the fish, more happy because Grandpa would have been proud of me.

I looked over my shoulder as I sat down in the float tube and prepared to kick paddle my way through the deep hole of water ahead. The little dogs were nowhere in sight. I felt bad that I could not do anything to help but was happy they were not following us into what would have been certain danger. Once they went back to the low water bridge someone would come along and rescue them, I hoped.

I floated silently through the water and stopped beside the tall rock. When I touched it, the mystical image of a rainbow-colored stained glass window appeared overhead. It was the same as the one in the Methodist church in the town where I grew up. My grandpa donated money to buy it after the seventy-five-year-old wooden structure burned down. He had both our names inscribed at the bottom in raised black letters. A rush of emotion caused a lump in my throat and my lower lip quivered.

"Look at that," I said as I pointed at the image.

"What?" Mike shaded his eyes with the palm of his hand and looked up in the sky.

"Don't you see the stained glass window?" He shook his head. He looked away and hooked another fish.

As quickly as it appeared, the image went away. I had seen it once before in a dream, but never in daylight. I started to ask Mike if he thought it might be my grandfather trying to communicate with me, but he was fighting a fish so his mind was on autopilot. A nice sized smallmouth jumped out of the water, shook his head, threw the lure and swam away.

"That fish would weigh three pounds," Mike said.

"Maybe half that much," I said. When I looked up again the image was gone. My eyes filled with tears as I remembered helping my grandfather work in the garden planting corn and helping him butcher a hog in the fall so we would have meat for the winter.

"What's wrong?" Mike asked.

I shook my head and looked away as I headed downriver. After we paddled through the Chimney Rock hole and were about half mile into our trip, we floated through a long ripple and headed into another long, deep hole of water.

"Let's camp here tonight," Mike said as he landed a goggle-eye the size of his hand. "We can go a little farther tomorrow. This place is full of fish!"

"It's not even noon and there are fish up ahead as well," I said, thinking we needed to go a little farther so we would not have to push so hard on Sunday, our last day on the river.

Anytime Mike was silent it was because he figured I was right, so we paddled through the quarter mile hole of water to the next riffle without anything else being said. To our delight, the next fast water chute was three feet deep and we rode the current without having to get out of the tubes. The river bottom was littered with boulders, some three feet tall and five feet around, a paradise for smallmouth bass. A swirling backwater eddy dropped off into a deep hole where a large fallen sycamore was lodged against a limestone bluff rising one hundred feet above the river. This was perfect cover for goggle-eye and sunfish, which we could catch and fry for dinner and breakfast the next morning.

A wide gravel bar covered with grayish-white pebbles ran parallel to the long hole of water and there was a spring near by where we would camp for the night. It was a paradise for me; I loved to be lulled to sleep by the sound of gurgling water. Mike was happy because on the first cast, the instant his baby Zara Spook hit the water close to a patch of lily pads, a big smallmouth at least five pounds inhaled the top water lure and leaped into the air. The fish shook his head from side to side, putting on a great acrobatic display. Mike released the old fish, sometimes called a mossback after a hard fought battle that tested his skill to land the fish on an ultra-light spinning reel with four-pound test line.

Setting up camp was simple. There is a lot to be said for traveling light and sleeping under the stars, except for mosquitoes, snakes, rainstorms, lightning and who knows what else.

I looked up at the wide blue sky and watched half dozen buzzards circle overhead, riding the thermal currents, something they can do effortlessly for hours without flapping their wings, due to nature's design of their long flight feathers.

"You think they know something we don't?" I asked; since buzzards mostly eat stuff that's dead.

Mike glanced up and shrugged his shoulders. His mind was on one track: catching fish. During the rest of the afternoon we landed at least fifty goggle-eye, sunfish and smallmouth bass. When the bite on artificial slowed down, we switched to crawdad tails and hellgrammites that we dropped alongside root wads and sunken rock ledges. The water was so clear we could see the goggle-eye and sunfish dart out from their cover and take the bait. The smallmouth were more wary. We cleaned a half-dozen fish for dinner, wrapped them in aluminum foil and laid them in our fire pit to bake.

We turned in at sundown with plans to walk, wade, and float our way to within three miles of our take out on Sunday. We would need to move along at a steady pace. I thought about seeing the stained glass window again and remembered the last time Grandpa and I floated the river. We fished very little as the trip was mostly him telling about family history and many things he had learned about the ways of the outdoor world.

Out of the clear blue Mike said, "What if this is our last fishing trip?"

I looked at him and frowned. "Hopefully it won't be. Why did you bring that up?" On occasion his mind had a tendency to wander off the beaten path.

He smiled. "Maybe being stalked by the buzzards all day had something to do with it."

I didn't respond, and he said nothing else, so I figured he had drifted back into his world of fishing the outer limit. He could be thinking about what lure to start with the next day or a big fish that got away. We did agree strongly on one thing, the power of positive fishing. If you thought you would catch a big fish, you had a better chance to do so than if you mindlessly made cast after cast while day dreaming about mundane things which had nothing to do with nature. We smugly thought there was a dividing line between city fisherman types who bought every tourist lure they could cram into their tackle box and those who grew up fishing. In my case, since I lived on the river as a kid and had a chance to learn from my dad, grandpa and uncle, who helped feed the family by fishing for food, I had an advantage.

I stared up at the sky until I saw the first star appear and not long afterward drifted off to sleep. Sometime in the middle of the night I awoke with a feeling I was being watched. When I opened my eyes, I saw something that almost caused my heart to leap out of my chest. I grabbed the flashlight beside my bedroll and jumped up to see what had invaded my space. It was one of the pups I thought we had left behind. His running mate, the little black dog, was curled up at the foot of Mike's bed.

Mike was on his feet in seconds. "What in the world is going on?"

"The pups are back," I said. "The white one scared me half to death. I was asleep and he licked my face."

Mike raised his hands up in the air. "What are we going to do with them now?"

When I sat down to think about a plan, the little white one crawled toward me on his belly and laid his head on my leg. As much as I hated to give in and be his friend, I patted him on the head. Then Mike made the fatal mistake of naming his new companion Blackie. In the dark of night, on a lonesome stretch of river, in the middle of the Ozark Mountains, we had adopted ourselves two little dogs for the remainder of our trip.

I tossed and turned the rest of the night, periodically looking over at my newfound friend, who was asleep with his head on the edge of my air mattress. I was up at dawn, built a fire, and made coffee. If I had not known better, I would have sworn the pups were companions we invited into camp or brought along on the trip. They were wrestling with one another and having the time of their lives. Little did we know the potential dangers up ahead. There were no roads for the next six miles, a lot of deep water, rugged terrain and worse than anything, cottonmouths. We couldn't backtrack upriver to the SUV since the vehicle would have already been moved to the take out spot. Our only option was to continue downriver.

"They'll ruin our fishing splashing in the water," Mike said, as we started downstream. I tried to get Whitey to ride on the air mattress mule or my lap in the Fish Cat, but he squirmed around and jumped off. So he and his brother Blackie trailed along the riverbank swam in the water and barked at endless blue and red dragonflies as they zoomed past the pups at thirty miles per hour. Because of our new liability, we decided to push on through rather than spend another night on the river. The danger was too great for our newfound friends. They were skinny as rails, and we had no extra food.

Even though the pups created a disturbance as they splashed along in the edge of the water, leaping in occasionally for a swim, Mike still caught plenty of fish. The trouble came after we had gone three or four miles to where the river narrowed, and we were faced with a long, deep hole of water. A towering bluff on the right and thick scrub brush on the left made it impossible for the pups to continue without danger. I paddled over to the bank and tried to get Whitey to join me on the Fish Cat. He ran away as if I was playing a game. Mike even laid down his fishing rod and made an attempt to rescue Blackie by holding out his last cracker. The pup got close enough to grab the food out of his hand then ran away from him as well.

Like many times when you think things have gotten bad as they can get, the horror I had been concerned about raised its ugly head. Swimming along the edge of the bluff with much of its body on top of the water in a stately way, was a dark brown cottonmouth, big around as my arm and four feet long. He was headed for the little dogs. Unaware of the danger, Whitey waded into the water toward the snake.

"Oh, Lordy," Mike said as he saw the snake at the same time. "Shoot him!"

The sound of Mike's voice stopped the snake from swimming farther up the river. He swished his pointed tail back and forth and slithered toward us. The river being so low, odds were this aggressive fella had not seen a human all summer. No doubt Mike and I didn't fit any part of his survival plan.

"If I shoot him and only wound him, he'll come after us," I said.

To my surprise, Mike made a snap decision that I would never have imagined in my wildest dreams. He paddled over and unsnapped the safety strap on the holster in my fishing vest, removed the revolver and like a charging bull headed for the snake that was closing in on our little dogs. They, of course, had no fear and were walking farther into the water toward the snake. When he was within 20 feet of his prey, the killer snake turned and stopped as if he was trying to stare him down. Mike leveled the revolver and fired. The bullet kicked up a spray of water a couple inches from the snake's head. The loud blast startled Mother Nature's creatures.

Caw, caw, caw, a crow cried as he flew across the river. A squirrel barked from up on the ridge. A buzzard flapped his big black wings and took flight from a dead tree limb on top of the bluff. The shrill call of a blue jay sitting on a low hanging branch of a sycamore warned of danger. Blackie barked and Whitey howled.

I wished I had a video camera to capture the scene because I would never see anything like it again, I hoped. The bullet from Mike's next shot hit the snake in the neck and the force blasted his head backwards. Suddenly, there was silence as we watched the twisting, turning body of a potential killer sink slowly into the deep clear water.

91

We picked up the pups and held onto them until we paddled through what we later referred to as the "Blackie and Whitey Trouble Hole." We let them out on the bank at the next gravel bar when it was safe for them to walk along beside us. On down the river, close to our take out, we ran across a family whose dog; a Coonhound named Lucky, had been bitten by a copperhead months earlier and died. When we told them our story, they adopted Blackie and Whitey on the spot. They still had a couple cans of Alpo dog food in the trunk of their car leftover from when they owned Lucky.

I've floated a lot of rivers but nothing compared to the likes of the trip Mike and I made on the upper Jacks Forks during dog days of summer, when we rescued Blackie and Whitey and left the river happy as we could be. As if Mike had not had enough after catching over hundred fish during the past three days, he read old issues of *In-Fisherman* as I drove on the way back to Kansas City.

Chapter 24

Boy Breaks Ice Swims to Safety

I walked up behind Vance Donavon, owner of the feed mill and patted him on the shoulder. "Bet you never thought you'd see me back."

Vance looked around and grinned. "Sure I did, you're tough as a pine knot."

"How thick is the ice?" I asked

"About seven inches. Thick enough nobody will fall through."

I knew what he was thinking about, but I paid him no mind.

"Everybody makes mistakes," I said.

During the summer, we fished for catfish and bluegill in the millpond. When it froze in winter, it became a gathering place for ice skaters. On this day, the news had spread that the ice on the mill pond was safe, since it was Saturday there could be fifty people and a dozen dogs show up to enjoy the day. There were already fifteen skaters and half dozen dogs. A couple of kids were roasting marshmallows over an open fire and drinking hot cocoa and it was only nine o'clock in the morning. My friend, Iver, who was holding onto an inner tube and being pulled around in a circle by Bob Peters, yelled at me and laughed, "Be careful you don't fall through the ice."

"Yeah, right!" I yelled back so I would be heard over the barking dogs and growling sound of the tube sliding on top of the ice. Iver fell off the tube and slid across the ice coming to a stop in a stand of frozen cattails at the edge of the pond, and I laughed.

I sat on a log close to the fire while I put my skates on. Another friend jumped out of his dad's pickup and walked up to remind me of the headline in the local newspaper the year before, which read, "Boy Breaks Ice, Swims To Safety."

The problem came about because after a couple days when the temperature got above freezing, the ice melted enough even though it froze again at night and was thick as before, however, it was rotten, a condition called honeycombed ice. What did I do? I walked out onto the pond and chopped a hole with an ax so I could fish. Without warning, the ice gave way, and I fell through.

Lucky for me the water was only about three feet deep, still I could not get out because my legs were buried in mud up to my knees.

Having a busy imagination my mind ran wild. The first thought being, I would freeze to death and even though snapping turtles were hibernated, if I was standing on one they just might get upset, come out of the mud and bite me. There were possums, raccoons, skunks and fox living in the tall grass and cat tails that could come out of hiding, it would be especially bad if they had rabbis.

Eventually, Bud Jones drove by, saw me waving and came to my rescue by throwing me a rope, which he tied onto the bumper of his pickup and pulled me out. I was so cold by the time I got home I was numb. Since that was the biggest news of the week, my accident was a front-page story. *Boy Breaks Ice Swims To Safety.* Only Bud and I knew I was stuck in the mud. He didn't tell anyone what actually happened and neither did I.

Chapter 25

Daydreaming My Way Through School Was
A Poor Way To Learn

During my freshman year in High School, my blonde headed friend the Tin Foil Girl seemed to like me more all the time. I judged that partly because of the lingering smile each time we looked at one another. I had not seen her since my mother and I moved to the river in the springtime. Imagine how delighted I was to see her after spending a summer with mainly outdoor creatures as friends.

One of my downfalls in school was daydreaming during class. As the teacher talked, I thought about things like I wished I was older so I could get a driver's license and take my soon-to-be girlfriend to an outdoor movie in a town close by. I wished I were back on the river living a life of leisure instead of doing homework. I wished my dad and uncle Clyde had not gone away, and my mother had not suffered so much sadness. Even back then I thought about writing a book giving myself a brother so I could vicariously be his friend.

Sad to say, I goofed off a lot and paid the price in later years. The only thing that kept my attention was fear of the teacher calling on me and me not having an answer. I played on the junior basketball team; I wasn't a star but I was good as most players. I hunted quail and rabbits after school and on the weekends. After I cleaned my game which mom fried 'em up and we ate them generally along with eggs, homemade biscuits sometimes apple pie. Where I truly shined was at shooting pool eight ball was my specialty. Fact is I got good enough to beat everyone in town.

My mother, being one of the best cooks around, picked up a job at Bunker Hill Retreat: a resort for teachers located ten miles downriver from Cardinal Acres where we lived the summer before. It was a beautiful camp with twenty housekeeping cabins located along the river. There was a main lodge with a few grocery items, picnic tables on a well-kept lawn and a large open-space shelter where people played shuffleboard and square danced on weekends. Since I had experience from square dances held in our barn, I was the official caller, which impressed the guest, especially the young ladies vacationing with their parents. Things could not have been more adventuresome and exciting for a fifteen year-old boy.

During the day I cut weeds, hauled away trash, shucked corn, and cleaned the fish I caught using crawdads, redfin minnows, and worms. Guests would show up early for lunch when they knew a mess of smallmouth bass was being served. When my chores were done, generally around noon, I would lead a few boys and girls up the river a half-mile to explore a cave. Anywhere from eight to ten of us young people paddled jon boats and canoes. There was a nervous disorder among the parents, watching their citified young folk go off into the wilderness with a boy who had the potential to be a bit wild. I timed our trip so we would see the spring that ran from the mouth of the cave's ebb. The water flowed forcefully each day at 2:00 PM and the event never failed to get the attention of my crowd. Back in the day, water was pure enough to drink out of the spring branch; I always took the first swallow to show the others it was safe.

One day, as I brought a half dozen kids back to camp from our cave exploration, I saw a dozen buzzards up ahead perched in a dead tree on top of a tall limestone bluff across the river from Bunker Hill camp. I jumped out of my jon boat and waved my arms to scare them. As my boat floated downstream I decided to show off, especially for the girls, and swim under a rock ledge a large flat part of the bluff that had broken loose ages earlier and created a structure shaped like a lean-to shelter.

I took a deep breath and started to swim though the underwater tunnel. Suddenly, there was a rush of horror unlike anything I had known, even worse than the cottonmouths I had encountered. A pile of driftwood had clogged the exit. My heart felt like it was beating in my throat. I scrambled backwards, scraping my arms and legs on sharp edges of the limestone rock as I struggled to escape my underwater tomb. Lord, I prayed, save me for the sake of my mother, she can't stand another death. By some miracle, I made it to the entrance, it felt like my lungs exploded as air rushed out when I screamed. I swam to the gravel bar, looked up at the sun and, for the first time, truly appreciated being alive.

"I thought you was supposed to come out the other end.'" A kid named Bobby said. "You're bleeding all over."

That was the last week of camp at Bunker Hill for the season. My mother and I moved back to town, and I started my sophomore year. I could hardly wait to see the Tin Foil Girl. The last time she was standing on the riverbank wind blowing in her long blond hair she looked pretty as a photo of a model. My greatest hope was she had not found someone during the summer she liked more than me.

Chapter 26

Sophomore Year Summersville High 1955

My sophomore year I played baseball and basketball, hunted wild game and caught fish for food, shot pool and goofed off a lot. My claim to fame happened during a baseball tournament at a neighboring town where I pitched a no-hit game against a talented team, which sent me to baseball camp the summer of my junior year. There I met the aging baseball hall of fame player Ty Cobb. He was a friend of the owner. I later turned down a chance to play minor league baseball because the pay was next to nothing. The odds of playing in the big league were remote, and I didn't want to ride a bus around the country and sleep in crappy hotels. Not at least checking it out was another mistake during my young life.

The baseball camp was located five miles downstream from Montauk State Park Fish Hatchery, close to Salem, Missouri. A spring, flowing an estimated 53,000,000 gallons daily, provided water for the hatchery breeding pools and formed the headwaters of Current River, a swift cold stream that flows though the Ozark Mountains for miles before running into the Black River. It was wild and scenic country teaming with fish, birds, wild animals and hundreds of caves. While I was in the Boy Scouts, I floated the one hundred mile stretch of the Current River in a canoe. The five-day journey was miserable; we almost were eaten alive by misquotes, badly burned by the sun, and lost most of our food the third day when we hit a log and turned over. I salvaged a jar of peanut butter and a can of pork-n-beans. Not all Boy Scouts are prepared.

On occasions, a baseball camp buddy and I would go to the breeding pools at the hatchery and, under the cover of darkness, catch a couple of rainbow trout that weighed six or seven pounds. We'd take them back to the baseball camp and tie them to the limb of a willow tree. The next morning, we would claim we caught the big fish by a bridge that crossed the river. A bunch of boys carrying fly rods, hoping to catch a prize fish big as ours, would rush to the river. None was ever successful. We used liver for bait during our nighttime fishing trips, which trout in the breeding pools liked because liver pellets were what the parks and wildlife people fed the big fish as a steady diet. Early on I cleaned a couple but they tasted too much like their daily diet to eat. A lot like goose liver you buy at the store.

Chapter 27

Uncle Ira's River's Edge Pool Hall

My friend Iver waved when Dad pulled up in front of the pool hall. I waved back. He flicked his tongue in and out like a snake and showed the wide gap in his front teeth. I would have never guessed by the end of the day he would be at deaths door, or that I would be responsible.

Ned, Lou and Sylvester, three of the oldest citizens, with a combined age of almost three hundred years, sat on a bench in front of the pool hall where they told stories and whittled the day away. They spoke to everyone who walked down the sidewalk and waved at people as they rode by on tractors, horses, cars and pickups. My best guess is they would say howdy and wave to people fifty times each day.

Iver stepped out the front door twirling a cue stick as if he was leading a parade. With a cocky grin he said, "Feelin' like you might win one today?" He had won six games in a row. I did not want him to make it seven. He was spending the night at our house and hearing him brag the entire time was not part of the plan.

"Go to it, boys," Dad said as he stepped out of the pickup, walked inside the pool hall and sat down in a chair at the head of the pool table.

Picked my favorite cue from the rack, one with my initials carved in the butt end. It felt sticky when I slid it through my fingers, so I poured talcum powder into my palm. The cue slid smooth as silk.

Ira, owner of the pool hall grabbed a grape soda from the cooler and a Baby Ruth bar from the candy case. He sat on a wooden bench with Ned, Lou and Sylvester who had shuffled through the door to watch the action. With everyone in place, it was time for the game to begin. I took a deep breath and told myself to relax. I had to win.

Iver chalked the tip of his cue stick as he walked to the head of the table. A loud high-pitched squeak filled the room. He continued the noise to irritate me.

"Rack 'em up. May the best man win." Iver had a sparkle in his eyes that made his unruly, curly red hair seem more colorful than usual. I wondered if he smeared some red cake coloring on it. He looked a lot like a clown.

Stay calm. I took my time and picked up the rack. I told myself nothing Iver said or did was going to bother me.

We both shot good pool when we were on our game. If the balls lay just right after a break, either of us could step up to the table and run an eight ball rack, five times out of ten. The only person in town who could beat us was Ira. He was a natural born pool shooter; he had excellent hand-eye coordination and the stroke of a professional. His reputation went as far as Kansas City, Little Rock and St. Louis. Challengers would stop in when they were in our neck of the woods to try and beat him. It was not unusual for a twenty-five dollar bet to ride on each game. You could count on one hand the number of times Ira had lost a pool game.

Born Dead on a Winter's Night

Ira bought the fancy tables from a guy retiring from the pool hall business. They were beautiful pieces of furniture imported from Germany. Ira referred to them as works of art. Their mahogany side panels had wild-eyed stags being chased by sleek, long-necked hounds carved in them. Pearls shaped like diamonds were embedded along the top of the railing. The balls rolled true over green felt cloth covering thick slate beds.

Ira opened the River's Edge Pool Hall after he hurt his back in the logging woods and could no longer do heavy lifting. It soon became the social gathering place for most of the men and a few brave women. The day the tables arrived from Chicago on a flat bed truck, it took half dozen men to haul them inside because the slate beds weighed two hundred pounds each. Along with my Dad, Ira was one of the smartest men I knew. How could it get any better than being able to shoot pool, drink grape soda, eat candy bars and peanuts every day without have to pay?

On Iver's lag to determine who got to break first, the ball rolled against the head rail and stopped. It was a perfect shot. "Nice one" I said. I can't do any better. Break 'em up." I stepped away from the table, looked up at the ceiling fan and watched the black wooden blades turn slowly as they pushed hot air around the room like they had ever summer for the past fifty years. I looked down when Iver groaned. I knew he did it on purpose to get my attention.

He took a deep breath and exhaled loudly, bent down and slid the stick back and forth through his fore finger a couple of times. He drove the cue ball into the rack and there was a loud "crash." I watched as a striped ball fell into the corner pocket and another one rolled into the side.

"Nice break," I said. Iver grinned, but didn't take his eyes off of the table. There were five stripes and the eight ball lying out in the open like sitting ducks.

"Nine in the corner," he called and drilled it into the pocket. Low English brought the cue ball back into perfect position on the twelve, which he shot in the side pocket. Next he dropped the eleven and easily made the last two stripes.

He had been Mr. Concentration shot after shot. Now with only the eight ball left on the table, he could not resist looking at me with a smile that ran ear to ear. He reminded me of a Halloween pumpkin.

"You've shot a good stick so far," I said. "Let's see how you do with the eight."

"Keep shootin' that way, Iver. You may beat me someday," Ira said as he winked at me and I winked back.

"That day's not far off," Iver said as he studied a bank shot in the side pocket.

"Tough shot you got there, son," Ned said.

Iver stepped away from the table and shook his head. "Not when you're a tough shooter like me."

I knew Ira and Ned's interruptions had broken Iver's concentration. He blinked a lot when he got nervous.

"What we got goin' here?" Leonard Thompson asked as he walked through the door. Taking off his green John Deer hat, he wiped the sweat from his forehead with the tail of his faded blue denim work shirt.

Iver looked up from the table and shook his head. "My gosh, Leonard. Can't you see I'm about to shoot?"

Leonard threw his hands up in the air and groaned as Iver bent down to line up his shot again. There was only a gnat hair of room for the eight to roll past my five ball and find the pocket without a deadly kiss.

"Damn it!" Iver yelled when the bank shot went wide and missed the side pocket by half an inch.

"Too bad," Ira said. "You could of won the game without Tommy firing a shot."

"Think I don't know that?" Iver snapped at Ira.

"You actually lucked out, son. You could have scratched as well as missed the pocket," Ned chuckled.

"I wanted to give Tommy a chance," he said. He picked up his Royal Crown Cola setting by the cue stick rack and drained the bottle with one long swig.

If I can shoot worth anything, I'll be okay. I told myself. All of the solid balls were out in the open if I just don't choke. I took a long deep breath to calm the quiver in my stomach.

I studied the table and talked out the strategy in my head. I'll put low English on the cue ball when I shoot the four. That will back it up for a simple shot into the side pocket on the three ball. Next I'll shoot the five in the corner pocket and the rest should be easy.'

I bent down and relaxed, got a good feel for the stick as I slid it through my forefinger and drilled the four ball into the corner pocket. The cue ball backed up and stopped in a perfect position. I shot the three and sank the remaining five balls down to the eight.

"Darn!" I yelled, when I cut the eight too thin, caught the corner of the pocket and rolled it toward the far end of the table.

"Got yourself a good leave, Tommy," Uncle Ira said as we watched the cue ball stop against the rail.

"Iver's got a lot of green between him and the eight ball," Leonard said as he looked at me and smiled.

Ned eased up out of his chair for a better view and said, "It's tough when your cue ball's frozen against the rail."

"Iver's made tough rail shots before, haven't you, son?" Sylvester said to Iver, as he was ready to shoot.

The cue ball barely brushed the eight, came off the rail too hard and rolled toward the right hand corner pocket, stopping a couple inches short. He left me an easy shot and the thrill of a win sounded loudly when the eight ball dropped into the leather pocket.

I jumped up in the air and yelled, "All right!"

"It was close," Iver said. "Could have gone either way."

Ned slapped Sylvester on the shoulder and laughed. "Close don't count except in horse shoes."

Iver took a couple of balls from the pocket and laid them on the table. "I'll rack and we'll shoot one more game, okay?"

"You boys can play again later," Dad, said as he got up out of the chair and walked toward the front door. I've got to pick up some feed from the mill and go check on an old cow ready to give birth."

I put my cue back in the rack, glad to leave the pool hall a winner for a change.

While Dad was in the mill picking up feed, Iver and I hurried to the pond, which was only fifty feet away. We caught a couple of grasshoppers and threw them into the water. Quick as a wink a bluegill came to the surface and the grasshoppers disappeared in a splash.

We ran to the pickup and climbed in the back with my dog Trouser when Dad yelled that he was ready to go. I sat down with my back against the cab and Trouser laid his head in my lap.

We left a cloud of swirling brown dust behind as we headed down a gravel road and ten minutes later pulled up in front of our white two-story farmhouse. When we walked into the kitchen there was a note on the table from Mom that she had gone to visit Aunt Maude and would not be home until dark. She said there was fresh baked cherry cobbler in the cupboard.

Iver and I scooped out a couple of bowls full and took our cobbler to the porch. We sat in a wooden swing and glided back and forth as we ate. We watched a pair of brightly colored wood ducks swim along the edge of the pond located a stone's throw away. A red-tailed hawk soared high above in the clear blue sky. A cardinal perched in an apple tree in the front yard and sang loudly, "cheer cheer cheer, whit-chew whit-chew, purty purty purty." Only the Devil himself could cause something to go wrong on such a beautiful day.

After we finished our cobbler and ice cream, I sat my bowl on the floor, leaped out of the swing and told Iver he might never win another game of pool in his entire life. That was all it took for him to jump out of the swing and onto my back. He rode me to the floor and yelled. "I got you last."

While I lay there, he ran to the other side of the porch and stood by the corner of the house, pushing the porch swing back and forth while he waited for me to come after him. When I fell, I skinned my elbow and it stung like fire. He poked his finger at me and laughed. I thought about how rough he had been and it made me mad. I jumped up, made a run toward him and pushed him so hard I shoved him off of the porch. On the way down he caught his chin on the edge of a sawhorse Dad had used to paint a flower box for Mom. Iver lay on his back, staring wide-eyed at the sky. He gasps for air and looked like he was almost dead.

"You okay Iver!" I yelled as I jumped down beside him.

Seconds later the screen door banged open against the side of the house. Dad stepped onto the porch and yelled, "What's goin' on boys? You tryin' to kill one another?"

I watched Iver's face turn blue. I wished lightening would strike me dead and put me out of my misery. I wanted to answer Dad, but the best I could do was point at Iver and hope a miracle would save him. Dad jumped down beside me, took one look and headed for the truck.

"I'm goin' after Doc," he yelled, as he ran to his pickup truck and backed out of the driveway. "Don't touch him," he shouted out the window as he wheeled out onto the road and headed toward town.

My mind ran wild. You've killed one of your best friends. People will hate you forever. You might be put in jail. I was tormented by my thoughts until dad returned with Doc Barnes. The night before when I crawled in bed I had a feeling something bad was going to happen.

Dad slid to a stop in the driveway and Doc jumped out of the cab on a run. One quick look at Iver, gasping for breath and Doc went into action. He looked at me with blue eyes flashing and said, "Get a pillow. I need it now!"

I rushed into the house, grabbed the yellow pillow with a blue embroidered duck on it off the couch and hurried back out the door. Iver started to breathe better right away after I handed the pillow to Doc and he slid it under Iver's neck to tilt his head back. At the same time, Doc flipped open the top of his black medicine bag. When it banged against the side of the leather case. Trouser jumped up from under a hickory nut tree and started to chase his tail, having a howling fit.

"It's a horse fly," I said after I figured out the trouble. When I looked back down I saw an awful sight. Doc had pushed the blade of a knife into Iver's throat. Blood filled the incision and that was the last I saw of the operation. I passed out and slumped to the ground. When I came to, Trouser was licking my face. Doc had inserted a silver tracheotomy tube into Iver's throat, and he was breathing through the hole. Tears streamed down his cheeks, which were pink again instead of blue. Doc and Dad loaded Iver in the back of the pickup to haul him to Doc's office. Doc put his arm around my shoulders and said, "Gettin' me a pillow real quick helped save Iver's life."

If it did or not, I didn't know. His saying it made me feel better. Iver never told anybody how the accident happened, and I sure as heck never did. No doubt about it, Doc saved Iver's life. It was a terrible experience for me. I could only imagine what it was like for Iver. It was the most scared I had ever been in my life.

Folks in small towns don't have much new news to talk about on a daily basis. So for a while after Iver's brush with death, I figured some folks talked about what they thought really might have happened and if it might have been my fault. Sure I was partly to blame. But like Doc said, I helped save Iver's life and that is what counts.

After the accident Iver's voice turned low and raspy like a croaking frog. Older kids make bullfrog noises and call him Froggy. Iver finally grew tired of the teasing and ended up in a couple of fights. After he beat the tar out of the school bullies, they picked on somebody else. I even fought one battle for him out of guilt for what I had done. Most of all, I did it because he was my friend.

Iver did not spend the night at our house anymore that summer. Probably just as well.

Chapter 28

Back at School Junior Year

When I saw Tin Foil Girl in the hallway on the first day of school, she said she was glad I survived my one hundred mile adventure floating the Current River. A smile and raised eyebrows told the tale. I was known for taking chances on the river, exploring caves, getting lost because I went too far into the woods, and other edgy things. I would be sixteen years old in December and get my driver's license. She would be sixteen in October, and since her dad owned the Chevrolet dealership she could drive any car on the lot. She made a habit of picking me up and we motored around the countryside, playing the radio full blast, Elvis, Little Richard and lots of cheating-heart-type tunes. I always wished I could sing better.

I was getting close to being a driver in December and could hardly wait to get my hands on the wheel. As luck would have it, Dan the Sheriff ordered a 1955 Ford Crown Victoria with a 400 horsepower engine, which, for some reason, he didn't accept. Maybe the town board didn't come up with the money or decided Dan was not responsible enough to be a high-speed driver. Anyway, the beautiful green and white hardtop sat on the lot for a couple of weeks before I had a serious discussion with my mother about the possibility of buying the car. We had a 1953 Dodge with over 100,000 miles. It was only a matter of time before big car repair trouble came calling.

I remember the day we walked into the Ford dealership to make a deal. My heart pounded at the thought of mother making a swap. Low and behold, she did. The list price on the Ford was $2,200 and the trade-in value on the Dodge was $150.00. The day I got my license, I could not resist seeing what the Ford had to offer and I was blown away. On a two-mile-long straight stretch of highway outside of town, the machine leaped to 120 miles per hour, after which I shut it down out of fear.

After Dan the Sheriff found out my mother bought the car, he saw me at the pool hall and said, "You're an accident waiting to happen. Odds are you'll not be able to keep it under 100 for any length of time."

I know him saying that had nothing to do with what happened to my friend Tommy, but I thought about it for years. Tommy and I and a couple of our friends went on a fishing trip one warm spring day. We decided to take two cars so we could haul more gear. On the way back to town, we were running at a high rate of speed on a gravel road and Tommy, who was driving the lead car, went around a curve too fast and ran off the road. He hit an oak head on. Suddenly the guy I had known longer than any other friend was dead. The crash shoved the steering wheel into his chest. There were the deaths of my father and my Uncle Clyde, and now my best friend Tommy was gone. I was only sixteen.

What is going to be next? I wondered over and over following the accident. There is something about carrying the casket of your best friend on a warm summer day, sun shining bright and birds singing in the background, that makes you realize the end of life can be waiting right around the corner.

Chapter 29

Summertime Blues

The last three summers had been the best of times. Fishing and guiding tourists, swimming in spring-fed rivers, exploring Mother Nature's gifts of bounty, calling square dances, escaping a watery grave, playing baseball, and roaming the countryside with Tin Foil Girl. I didn't feel like doing any of that anymore after losing the people I loved. I wanted to do something mindless to help me forget. I was offered a labor-intensive job and snapped it up.

A farmer had a five-acre field covered in oak tree saplings called sprouts. The only way to prepare the land so it could grow crops was to chop them out of the ground with an ax. It was perfect for my healing: working under a blazing sun, sweat running in my eyes, swinging an ax, digging into the ground. Thirty days after I started, the field was cleared, and it was time to cut and bale hay. My job was to follow the baler and make sure nothing went wrong. Sometimes the twine holding the hay together broke, and loose hay dumped out onto the ground. Once we had enough hay for a load, I lifted seventy-pound bales onto the flatbed of a truck and stacked them ten feet high. Even though it was a relief to get in the cab of the truck out of the sun, once I got inside the barn to unload it was even hotter, over 100 degrees. I was covered in hayseeds that stuck to the sweat, my eyes were stinging and my throat dry.

Once hay season was over, I felt I had punished myself enough, I went back to my old ways, shooting pool, fishing ponds and rivers, taking float trips and enjoying the healing way of nature.

Chapter 30

Senior Year Time Flies

I went back to school playing baseball and basketball, daydreaming about the stuff I would do when the year was over. Now that Tin Foil Girl and I both had access to cars, our world became one of exploration in assorted hidden-away places. Since we lived in the country we had lots of options; dead end roads by the river, the graveyard, log roads used by trucks that hauled timber to the sawmill, and endless other deserted areas. Some had brush piled up so high only wild animals and I were aware of the entrance. I dare not go into detail about how compatible Tin Foil Girl and I became except to say we were close.

Our Ford Crown Victoria with the 400 horsepower engine only got 12 miles per gallon. Not significant though, considering gas was only twenty cents a gallon.

I thought about Tommy and visited his grave often. It was as if he came along in spirit on many of my escapades, particularly during a near-death experience the day we explored Leatherwood Cave, a cavern located a couple miles from the Jacks Fork River. Dub Terrell was a new boy in town and decided to join us hoping to become a member of the group. He was crawling through a small space in front of me and fell off of a ten-foot high ledge into a pool of icy cold spring water. He almost died of hyperthermia before we could rescue him. Tommy would not have allowed something so stupid to happen, I thought.

When school was out and our graduating class of thirteen members, now reduced by one, were let loose to explore the world, I hung around town, because I was hooked on Tin Foil Girl. In addition to her looks, she was smarter than me, which I figured would be helpful in the long run. She played the piano and could warn me when I was about to do something stupid without being bossy. She had the magic touch a chosen few had that made people want to be her friend.

Chapter 31

The Best Bird Dog In The Ozark Mountains

Dad and Uncle Ira loved to hunt quail. They were two of the best shots in the county and usually brought home their limit of birds. But what they were most competitive about was who had the best bird dog. Uncle Ira owned pointers and crossbreeds and they were always males. He only did it to be different as best I could figure. He always named his dogs Hopalong, after a favorite cowboy character he listed to on the radio when he was a kid. He called them Hop for short. Anytime my dad talked about Uncle Ira's dogs the words hardheaded and long ranging came into play.

The bird dogs Dad owned were black and white English setters and they were always females named Lucille. His reason was simple. "She dogs are smarter than males and easier to train, he would say, and my mother would giggle every time she heard him say it."

There was a good reason why we had some of the best quail hunting in the Ozark Mountains. Quail primarily eat grain and acorns and require water close to where a covey would range. We had a plentiful supply of everything including an abundance of ponds, rivers and lakes. Farmers planted a lot of corn and would leave a few rows along the edge of their fields for quail to eat. There were wooded areas filled with oak trees that shed a plentiful crop of acorns. Brush and blackberry vines that matted the fencerows provided safety from predators and shelter from winter storms. In short, our country was a quail paradise. Shotguns and bird dogs were traded back and forth as frequently as a rooster in the barnyard-switched hens. The ideal birddog had a nose that could pick up a scent and track down birds even if they were on the run. A good dog would root around in a thicket, splash into the water after a cripple or a kill, honor another dog on point, never get close as to flush the birds and always obey a masters call. A perfect dog had a soft mouth and would retrieve a bird without ruffling a feather. I learned early on that even normally sane and generally responsible men would go to great lengths to find a good dog. It was his mission to own the best bird dog in the county that drove Uncle Ira to the extreme. Ira was smart as a whip in most ways, but when it came to having bird dog swapin' sense, Dad said he seemed to have little to none. Quail are not easy to hit and most of those who hunted them for meat used a Winchester automatic 12 gauge shotgun with an improved cylinder bore so the shot pattern would be wide spread. Dad and Ira took great pride in sporting a Model 42 Winchester pump 410 gauge with a modified bore. Anyone who could bag a limit of quail with a small gauge shotgun had to be quick on the uptake and dead on their fluttering prey when they pulled the trigger.

"Time for breakfast," Mom yelled up the stairs.

"Be right down," I shouted back.

I sat on the edge of the bed and looked out the window at the pale winter sun rising above the rooftop of the corncrib, a gray weathered building my grandfather built from hand-hewn logs when he moved to the Ozark Mountains in 1900's. A layer of frost that covered the rusted tin roof reflected the morning sun and sparkled like millions of tiny diamonds. I stared at the gate that led into the barn lot and remembered how on another cold winter day, at the urging of my friend Iver, I tried to lick a piece of ice off of the metal latch and my tongue got stuck. I panicked and jerked my head back when I realized I was trapped, leaving a piece of soft pink skin on the gate. My tongue was so raw for the next couple of weeks nourishment had to come from milk sucked through a straw. I was 6 years old at the time; I'm not so easy to fool now that I'm older.

I was so excited about hunting with dad and Ira on opening day of quail season that I slept fitfully during the night. My job was to carry the dead birds and keep a close eye on where the singles set down after a covey was flushed. And I was anxious to see Ira's new bird dog work the field. He claimed it was one of the best dogs in the county, even though it was a crossbreed and looked a little bit different. I jumped out of bed and started to dress for a cold winter day. I slipped on two pairs of socks, long john underwear, and my tan hunting pants with a double layer of cloth that covered the front of my legs to protect me from the thorn bushes.

"What you doing?" Dad yelled. "Ira's ready to hit the field and show off his new birddog."

"Be right down," I said as I tied my boots and looked at myself in the mirror. I ran my fingers through my long wavy brown hair, put on a red flannel shirt, bright orange hunting cap and headed for the stairs.

When I walked into the kitchen Dad and Ira had already started to eat and were having a conversation about who had the best bird dog of all time. It was more of the same old lingo about pointing, backing and retrieving birds. Even though I had heard it many times it was always exciting to hear again, especially on opening day.

"So you've got another new dog," Dad said as he looked at me and winked, then forked a piece of gravy covered ham into his mouth and washed it down with a swig of black coffee."

It was easy to tell when Ira was going to be defensive even before he said a word because he would tilt his head back and narrow his eyes.

"I'd mind ya to hold off any comments until you see him hunt. He's a mix between a Weimaraner and a Brittney Spaniel and doesn't look like your average run of the mill breed."

That made Dad laugh. "I can hardly wait to see the critter. I guess you've named him Hopalong as usual?"

"Nope. Haven't named him anything yet. I figured I'd let a name come natural once he starts to hunt."

I looked at Dad and he grinned from ear to ear.

117

In preparation for our exposure, Ira could not resist giving us a bit more description. "Like I say, the dog looks a little out of the ordinary. He's got short legs, a long body, thick reddish brown and white hair." When Dad and I looked at one another and laughed, Ira said, "The proof is in the pudding. You'd do well to wait until you see the dog hunt before a judgment is rendered."

"I suppose you know the fella well who owned the dog?" Dad said and gave me a wink. "No doubt he claimed the dog could smell a covey of quail all the way to the next county."

I gobbled down my last bite of biscuit when Ira pushed away from the breakfast table and said, "Like I told ya. The hunt will tell the story."

As we walked across the yard toward Ira's brand new red Ford Pickup, we saw his dog bouncing up and down on the seat. When I got a closer look, I started to laugh. Ira's description could only conjure up in the mind a fraction of the way the dog actually looked.

We put Dad's dog Lucille and Ira's new found fury treasure in the bed of the pickup truck and headed for the field. Dad's question along the way was if Ira saw the dog hunt before he forked over the money. Rather than answer Dads question Ira pointed at a flock of geese overhead and mentioned they seemed to be late heading south.

When we arrived at the field to hunt we got out of the cab and the dogs jumped from the truck bed. Uncle Ira's new dog made a beeline for the fencerow, jumped a rabbit and disappeared as he chased it into the woods.

"I didn't know good bird dogs would mess with rabbits," Dad said. "If they jump one they don't give chase and bark."

Ira looked the other way and shook his head.

"I think I know what to name your new dog," I said, remembering a character in a comic book I had read. "How about Zig Zag. Call him Zig for short."

At that point I might have said we should name the little fella the devil and Ira could have cared less.

Born Dead on a Winter's Night

We walked in silence along the edge of a cornfield for a ways and stopped when Lucille went on point. Out of nowhere, Zig ran past us and flushed the covey of birds. Ira took a wild shot and knocked one bird down. Soon as it hit the ground, Zig grabbed it and started to chew on it like it was his supper. Ira yelled and ran after the little dog. Once again he disappeared into the woods with the quail in his mouth. By now Zig was no longer at the top of Ira's best birddog in the county list.

As we continued the hunt, Zig appeared again fifteen minutes later at the end of a cornrow. This time he had something black in his mouth dragging it toward us. It was too big to be a crow and couldn't be a skunk because there was no white strip. As we watch in amazement the wind blew up a terrible smell that was like a mixture between rotten eggs and sour milk. When Zig got closer Dad said, "It looks like your birddog's found a dead buzzard."

"What are those little white things moving around on top of its feather?" I asked as I cocked my head to one side for a better view?

"Those would be maggots, Son," Dad said as he pinched off his nose with his fingers and walked away.

Uncle Ira hurried over and snapped a leash on Zig's collar, led him to the pickup truck and shut him up inside the cab. Dad and I agreed there was no need to say nary another word about Zig. When Ira joined us again Dad struck up a conversation about how much he liked Ira's new truck and I said red was my favorite color.

As we hunted the rest of the field, Lucille pointed a couple of coveys. Dad and Ira got half dozen birds each and we decided to call it a day, mainly because Ira's heart wasn't in the hunt any longer. He was too beat down about Zig.

As we walked toward the truck the sun was shining brightly, I noticed the cab looked like it was filled with spider webs. When Ira saw it he started to run. When he got close enough to tell for sure what had gone wrong he yelled at the top of his lungs, "Zig. What have you done?" The dog gone wrong had ripped part of the headliner out of Ira's shiny new truck and what looked like spider webs were shreds.

To make a long story short. Dad told Uncle Ira as a Christmas present, he would give him the pick of the liter next time Lucille had pups. He would also help train the dog so Ira could stop searching all over the county for a better birddog. Even though it turned out Zig was not a good birddog, Ira's daughter Jeannie adopted him. The little rascal was so talented he could stand on his hind legs and bark out a tune that sounded like jingle bells.

Chapter 32

Central Methodist College

Summer passed in regular fashion after high school graduation. I zoomed around the countryside in the high-powered Ford with Tin Foil Girl and friends who liked living on the edge. I floated and fished the Jacks Fork, Current and Eleven Points rivers, wild and scenic streams now part of the Ozark National Scenic Riverways. I worked in the hay fields and set pins at the bowling alley on occasions to make extra cash. I shot pool, explored caves, sneaked around and smoked cigarettes. When I was younger I included grapevines and corn silks. Grapevines made my tongue sore and corn silks left a taste in my mouth like burnt leaves. The only benefit being they were free.

A friend convinced me I should go to college rather than hang around a small town, so off to Central Methodist College at Fayette, Missouri I went. It was the best thing I could have done.

My backyard when I was a kid.
http://theozarkmountains.com/ozark_mountins.htm

Dogs I Have Known

Sad dogs don't iive as long as people.

Trouser – Basset Hound
1939-1947
Summersville, Missouri

Mr. Nose -Beagle
1948-1957
Summersville, Missouri

Misty – Cocker Spaniel
1957 – 1961
Springfield, Missouri

Kelly – Irish Setter
1961 – 1965
Roeland Park, Kansas

Sunny – Australian Shepherd
1997-2003
Overland Park, Kansas

Biscuit – Australian Shepard
2001 – 2012
Overland Park, Kansas

Cooper – Australian Shepherd
2009 – Present
Overland Park, Kansas

Hard to imagine anyone giving such a beautiful animal away. Cooper and I are at Kaw Point Park located at the confluence of the Missouri and Kansas Rivers. We are on one of 42 commutative stones, each engraved with the names of members who were on the two and one year, 8,000-mile Lewis & Clark expedition 1804–1806.

During the bicentennial 2004 -2006. I played Silas Goodrich, expert fisherman. The photo of Cooper and I was taken on one of the coldest days of the year – I was five degrees below zero.

Cooper is a comfort dog that visits Alzheimer's patients. Smiles light up the room when Coop walks through the door.

Snowy – mixed breed
1998-2014
Bonner Springs, Kansas

Found abandoned during a snowstorm at a gas station by daughter Jeannie. It was rare those who saw the unusual looking sweet boy that they didn't say, "What kind of dog is that?" Gone but never forgotten.

Abby – Mountain Bernese
1998-Present
Boston, Massachusetts

Our daughter Janet's family's Mountain Bernese, a beautiful animal with a calm disposition. Featured walker is the infamous Tin Foil Girl. The setting is a record 108 inches of snow in Boston winter of 2015. Growing up in the Ozark Mountains the woman has a pioneer spirit, when there is something she wants' to do, she does it!

Rogues Gallery

Names of people worthwhile I have known along the way. I did not included their last names in case I do something wrong and the Authorities are looking for character witnesses.

Mary-Lane K, Mike O, Jim M, Burt M, Tom M, Pat M, Larry B, Diane D, Lorie D, Ryan D, Amy D, Jo D, Dave A, Brian A, Bonnie A, Lisa A, Roger (Henpeck) A, Dewy A, Donnie A, Nub and Eunie A, Paul M, John K, Chris O, Mitch O, Martin O, Steve C, Pam C, Jon B, Mark A, Deb C, Ed H, Deb H, Johanna L, Tim G, Gregg G, Goeff G, Mike B, Sam G, Dewayne K, Chris K, Cris S, Glen, Jeannie E, Anthony O, Royal O, Lisa O, Nick E, Tom M, Brent F, Jonathan B, Samuel B, Clayton H, Dennis W, Robert W, Tom M, Deborah S, Julie H, Carolyn K, John M, Kevin Fewell, Katherine H, Lynne S, Al Moon, Cheryl Moon, Janet C, Jake C, Lauren C, Denis C, Kathrine C, Dennis C, Nick E, Mike T, Bruce, N, Stacy E, Fawn Smith, Cirene M, Susan C, Craig T, Mike C, Laura C, Jessica C, Ed H, Neil S, Lynn W, Scott N, Bernie N, Tin Foil Lady, (10) Dogs … **probably more but I'm running out of paper.**

Thanks for being a reader. Hope you enjoyed my memoir maybe learned a thing or two about what it was like growing up back in the day before technology replaced reality! If you want to Tweet, post on Facebook or use the old fashion means word of mouth that you got good vibes from my stories I'll appreciate your effort. One of my goals writing this stuff was to possibly influence kids that there is more to life than having a cell phone attached to one of their limbs most of their waking hours.

https://www.linkedin.com/pulse/commentary-social-networking-rolland-love

Rolland

About The Author

Rolland Love is the author of short stories, novels, a bestselling computer book and an award-winning cookbook. He created and presents workshops on journaling, writing, storytelling and life history for children and seniors. He is a speaker, has appeared on talk shows, and publications have written about his Mark Twain writing style.

Rolland was a re-enactor with the Lewis and Clark bicentennial expedition and played the role of Silas Goodrich, expert fisherman. He created a monologue about the adventure, which he presents to schools, libraries, retirement centers and civic groups.

Love co-founded a company that published a software series dealing with health education for young adults. He also directed the Respiratory Care department at Barnes Hospital, a twelve hundred-bed teaching institution affiliated with Washington University in St. Louis.

Rolland is available as a motivational speaker, presents a monologue about his Lewis and Clark adventure and a workshop about Creative Writing. For more information, Google Rolland Love

Books By Rolland Love
Blue Hole
River's Edge (sequel)
Toe Tags & TNT
Born Dead on a Winter's Night
http://tinyurl.com/ogxxlup
http://ozarkstories.com

Rolland Love

Short Stories
40 Published Titles
http://tinyurl.com/j5mbhlu

Free Short Stories
First Camping Trip With Dad http://tinyurl.com/qbovz44
Adrift on the Missouri River http://tinyurl.com/qcr5gjs

Authoring System Imastory
http://www.imastory.com
http://tinyurl.com/kfemmg5 (Reviews)

Facebook:
https://www.facebook.com/rolland.love
https://tinyurl.com/KCLIVE41 More Love

Twitter:
@Rollandlove

Fishing Stories (90) Minute Audio:
http://tinyurl.com/3v3qabq

Johnson County Community College "It's Our Community"
http://tinyurl.com/mfxuut8 (30 Minute Video)

Love On The Trail With Lewis & Clark
http://tinyurl.com/jpsqzna (50 Minute Video)

Websites of Interest:
How to play marbles http://tinyurl.com/pn3ve3n
How to build a rabbit trap http://tinyurl.com/jjc4fuw
I feel things then they happen http://tinyurl.com/hr75kad
Premonition http://tinyurl.com/zucl3zt
Intuition http://tinyurl.com/jncs5mm

Made in the USA
Middletown, DE
25 August 2019